BLⓄⓄD CRIMINALS

BL☣☣D CRIMINALS

Living with HIV in 21st Century America

Jonathan W. Thurston

Weasel Press

Blood Criminals: Living with HIV in 21st Century America
Jonathan W. Thurston

Copyright © 2019 Jonathan W. Thurston
Cover photo, "Processing" by Nolyn Voyd. Model C. L. Methvin. Photo editing by
Justin Battista. Cover design by Weasel.

ISBN-13: 978-1-948712-50-7

Weasel Press
Manvel, TX
www.weaselpress.com

Printed in the United States of America
10 9 8 7 6 5 4 3 2 1

Book design by Jonathan W. Thurston and Weasel

The author has made every attempt at checking the validity of website information, but neither the publisher nor the author takes any responsibility for any errors in the accuracy of this information after publication. Neither the publisher nor the author has any control over these third-party websites.

For Dustin

If ever we are nature's, these are ours; this thorn
Doth to our rose of youth rightly belong;
Our blood to us, this to our blood is born.

–WILLIAM SHAKESPEARE,
FROM *ALL'S WELL THAT ENDS WELL*, ACT 1, SCENE 3

A night with Venus, a lifetime with Mercury.

—ANONYMOUS, C. 16TH CENTURY, REGARDING SYPHILIS

CONTENTS

Author's Note

There are a few conventions I employed throughout this book that I want to make explicit from the get-go. Each of these conventions serves a journalistic or ethical purpose.

Except for public figures, all people living with HIV in this book have pseudonyms throughout the text. A few people related to people living with HIV also sometimes choose to have a pseudonym here. I respected these wishes whenever possible, and I did this to ensure not only that I was not publicly disclosing their status but also to prevent them from being criminalized for their coming forward with their stories.

Also, in most cases, I refer to the human immunodeficiency virus (HIV) as a sexually transmitted infection, not a disease. I have adopted the rhetoric that claims seeing HIV as a disease implies there are some kinds of visible, recognizable symptoms, whereas infection allows for an interpretation that HIV can live well beneath the skin. Many writers and activists still debate this distinction, but, for the sake of consistency, the term in this book will be sexually transmitted infection or STI.

And without further ado, thank you for reading.

Introduction

How many sex partners have you had in your life? Can you count them on one hand? How about two? How about so many you can't remember?

How long did you know these sexual partners? Were you in a relationship, or was this a hookup?

Where did you have this sex? Was it in the bedroom? The shower? The kitchen? The car? The park? A club?

Did you use protection? Every time? *Every* time?

Why not? Did you even trust the person?

Did you at least ask for their records?

Why not?

If you are diagnosed with HIV in the 21st century, these are just some of the questions you will be asked by your doctor, nurse, and case manager. They hand you some pamphlets, and, suddenly, your life changes, and you can't help but shake the feeling that maybe they think it's your fault, that you were asking for it with your decisions.

Some of these questions might be asked by a judge or law enforcement officer. Whether you're trying to sue the person who gave it to you or they're the ones trying to sue you—even though you didn't know you had it—you'll have these questions in front of you. Ask the people who are listed on online sex offender sites who were accused—but not convicted—of spreading HIV. Or ask the people who are in jail because they spat on someone while infected with HIV.

These questions will even be asked by your friends and family. Some will feel bad for you. Some will think you're disgusting. Some will even try to lecture you. Most importantly, they'll want to know, "Who did this to you?" They want to castrate him and prosecute him and hate him and call him out for the monster they see him to be.

And you? You just want to hold him. You want to be held by him. He was scared you wouldn't want to be with him if he told you. That doesn't make it right, but it doesn't make you hate him. Now more than ever, you need love. You need connection. You need to feel like you're not worthless, like you're not "just a slut," like you're not unclean.

When I was diagnosed in 2015, these were all questions I was asked. Call me to the stand.

It was my second boyfriend ever, my third ever sexual partner. I could count on one hand my number of partners by that point.

It was a monogamous relationship. I loved him with all my heart, and I thought we were made for each other.

We had sex whenever we wanted, and we did not always use protection.

Why?

Because I trusted him when he told me he was negative.

I did not ask for his medical records.

Because I trusted him.

But I don't hate him.

Living with HIV in 21st century America is incredibly different from what it was like living with it back in the 80s, when the AIDS epidemic first entered the stage. The death rate, at least here in the United States, is significantly lower than it was back then. The treatments are wonderful, able to keep you living as long as anyone else and just as healthy, too. The drugs are so strong that they can completely eliminate the risk of transmission. Better treatments, and even cures, are being investigated tirelessly in laboratories around the world! And yet, myriad problems have arisen: lack of access to healthcare that can cover the meds, side effects from the drugs themselves, courts and police departments labeling people like me "biohazards," disclosure laws that work to criminalize people living with HIV, and a cultural stigma that is so deeply embedded in the American psyche that suicide is one of the leading causes of death for people living with HIV.

I have faced this kind of stigma for years, and it's come from everyone: family, friends, colleagues, coworkers, doctors, nurses, and people I was interested in seeing romantically or sexually. It's everywhere. But my project here is not about telling my own story. No, this is not a memoir. Instead, this is a cultural exposé, one about the people living with HIV in America. Despite that national focus, even, HIV is very much a *global* concern. Seeing the work put in by the Global AIDS Network and similar initiatives is testament to that fact. By limiting this work to just American issues, I do not mean for a second to say other nations are not suffering worse than we are. However, if I can help you, the reader, to understand just one piece of the HIV/AIDS global puzzle, that is a success to me.

While I have transcribed what are now hundreds of pages of interviews for this project, I focus on the lives of eight specific people across America. They have been renamed throughout for anonymity, and I use these eight real-life narratives as stepping stones, moving out to talk about the issues at large: sex education, diagnosis, disclosure laws, criminalization, insurance, medication, and even dating while HIV-positive. Everyone's lives with HIV are different, yes, but many of the experiences share commonalities. There are trends, patterns that mark people living with HIV as part of a connected group that could only be called a culture (or at the very least, a cultural network).

The organization of this book, therefore, follows a very specific structure. The five chapters follow these people's lives from way before the potential for diagnosis, especially sex education; to the moment of diagnosis and all its complications; to the labyrinthine policies and procedures of healthcare, case management, and insurance; to the myriad ways that legal and judicial systems, law enforcement officers, and prisons work to criminalize people living with HIV; to the real-life horrors of dating and sex while you're HIV-positive. Inside each chapter, there is a section devoted to each of the major figures in the book. And, while the book does focus on these eight specific people, they all serve as points of departure for larger societal concerns. What happens to these eight individuals is symptomatic of problems in higher structures, not just in the individuals themselves.

This book is not a memoir, as a result. It is a work of

journalism, and I want to thank all the people who kindly allowed me to interview them for this book: the doctors, nurses, medical scientists, journalists, authors, professors, program directors, case managers, historians, lawyers, politicians, people living with HIV, and, sadly, people who have lost others to HIV. As someone living with HIV myself, I cannot pretend not to have a bias with this book. I simply can't. All the same, I will try to limit my presence within the body of this work, at least until the epilogue. My purpose is to present all of this information to you, these stories, and let you do with it what you will. Of course, it is my hope you will reach the end of this book with a little more knowledge than what you started with, and I hope that knowledge informs your thinking about people living with HIV. These are all real people, and that's part of what makes so many of these accounts terrifying, even to me. Again, though, this is not any one person's story.

It's the story of America and the people whose very existence can make them criminals, the incriminating evidence a tenth of a millimeter below the skin.

1 / *Education*

Alex and Derek

Back in the 1980s—a time of neon lights, *Gremlins*, *Pac-Man*, and the sensationalized struggle between Magic Johnson and Larry Bird—a disease emerged. It was known first as the gay-related immunodeficiency disease, or GRID. In some circles, the name for the disease became even more targeted, naming it for four specific risk groups, Haitians, heroin addicts, hemophiliacs, and homosexuals: the 4H disease. In 1982, the Center for Disease Control (CDC) gave a name to the condition that had already begun taking lives throughout America as well as other parts of the world: Acquired Immune Deficiency Syndrome, or AIDS. By 1986, however, scientists from both the Pasteur Institute and the National Cancer Institute finally discovered the cause for the disease, and an international committee named it the human immunodeficiency virus, or HIV.

What started out as a disease that caused a small handful of deaths in the early 80s quickly transformed into what we call the AIDS epidemic. By 1992, there were over 200,000 deaths in America alone due to HIV/AIDS, and by 2000, despite the advent of medications that could control the progress of the virus, 460,000 people had become victims. Sexual education programs at both primary and secondary schools have incorporated discussion of sexually transmitted infections into the curriculum. Many medical clinics now offer free testing and condoms, in an effort to control the spread of the virus. In 2019, the medications that exist are remarkable: they can prevent contraction of HIV, *and* they can prevent its transmission to someone else. However, public awareness of these treatments is limited.

In some ways, HIV exists in popular culture only to show how it is restrictively a *past* phenomenon, no longer relevant today. The acclaimed musical *RENT* features many HIV-positive characters, including one who dies by the musical's climax, but it places HIV/AIDS strictly in the 80s. HIV has entered popular comedy as well, with the form of dark humor often making jokes about how short life is if you have HIV, such as this one found online, "How do you turn a fruit into a vegetable? AIDS." Perhaps then, it is no surprise that people in the 21st century do not consider HIV a serious concern. But to the over one million people living with HIV/AIDS in this country, it *is* serious. While they can—usually—keep their health going strong, they deal with coldness from doctors, discrimination from work, criminalization from law enforcement officers, and suicide "requests" from the dating world.

By the early 2000s, HIV was largely a verboten topic, only to come about in the sex education programs offered at middle and high schools across the country, and even that has been met by some with criticism. Lori Cole, executive director of the conservative activist group Eagle Forum, said that teaching topics like STIs and contraception provides teens "a means to live an unhealthy lifestyle." Now, America has two major types of sex education: abstinence-only and comprehensive. Comprehensive sex education is called such because it teaches other means of preventing pregnancy and STIs than just abstinence: condoms, medication, and even different sexual practices. But even for places that have taught comprehensive sex education, the curriculum has often been minimal, whether in terms of time spent or the level of detail. In Flint, Michigan, this is no exception.

Alex Gardner, a high school student in Flint in the early 2000s, remembers his limited sex education now that he's 31. Founded in 1991, Mott Middle College High School was a school of two to three hundred students, and it is nestled inside the Mott Community College. Right across the street from the Community Gospel Church, it is not difficult to see what shaped the community's code of ethics. When the school taught sexually-transmitted infections, it was only out of a sense of obligation. HIV in particular, the "gay disease," was only mentioned in passing. "I remember hearing about it," Alex says, "but it was only for a single hour on a single day and never heard about again." His parents were never around to talk to him about sex education either. But of course, he still lived a fairly normal teenage life. He was on the school's chess team and the wrestling team for a couple of years until he hurt his back. He played Dungeons & Dragons almost religiously, and he had decent grades. On the weekends and during the summers, he would mow lawns for work. He even developed a social life through local fandoms. The lack of comprehensive sex education did not really affect him, he thought. He was not sexually active at the time anyway.

For Derek Williams, who was the same age as Alex and would move to Michigan shortly after high school, his middle and high schools in Norfolk, Virginia gave HIV only marginally more attention. HIV was "taught through a 'mandatory' school course named 'Family Life,' which was a two-week course every year unless a student had a signed permission slip from their parents omitting them from said course." The course was offered as a unit in the annual physical education class from grades five to ten, and it focused on general sexual intercourse. Students saw the anatomy of sexual organs and learned what different STIs looked like. The program taught both safe sex methods and abstinence. HIV was just one of the topics they touched upon. Walking away from these kinds of programs, Derek knew that HIV hampered the immune system's ability to fight off infection, making it easier to become infected with illnesses as well as making recovery time much longer. But he still didn't know what HIV really entailed, what treatments existed, or even the virus' history.

These kinds of stories are far from rare. The closer that one looks at sex education in the late 90s and early 2000s, the more one sees how terrifying portrayals of HIV were. Laura Lape, who also attended high school in the early 2000s, says in an online forum, "When I was a freshman, we had an abstinence program take over our health class for a week. One week we had to act out STIs and I was assigned chlamydia. On the last day, the teacher dimmed the lights and had us write out a letter explaining to our friends and family that we had just been given the news that we had AIDS, and explained how we had contracted it. After an hour of people crying in class and thinking about death, she tried to encourage us to keep that letter with us. No one did and most of us threw it away before we left the room." The University of Washington's Teen Aware program features a PowerPoint-based lesson that shows graphic photos of various STI symptoms, called "What's Up Down There?" Cody Sigel, MPH, frowns upon this kind of fear- and shame-based pedagogy, stating, "Inducing fear is not an effective way to promote sexual health risk reduction. Showing images of symptomatic genitals might lead some youth to believe that if their own genitals do not look like those shown in the image, they and their partner must not be infected with an STI. For some students, these graphic and disturbing pictures are the first realistic images they have seen of genitals. This negative approach pathologizes sexual activity instead of promoting positive sexual health and personal responsibility." Yet these kinds of horror stories persist. Especially abstinence-only programs employ the rhetoric of shame and fear to convince teens not to have sex. HIV becomes less of a biological virus and more of a divine punishment.

And for people like high-schoolers Alex and Derek, fear-based sex education helped them associate these STIs with a kind of errant sexuality. Only "bad" people got HIV. If you weren't a prostitute or actively seeking a virus, then you probably wouldn't get anything, right? Accurate information about HIV just wasn't really accessible, which affected their own sexual habits and behaviors. As Kekla

Magoon says in *Sex Education in Schools*, proponents of comprehensive sex education focus on the fact that "knowledge leads to safe choices, and ignorance leads to risky behavior." And if you don't have access to accurate information, then you can't make safe choices. Teens like Alex and Derek weren't really told about safe choices and what the risks really looked like, and that hurt them in the long run.

This isn't just a problem at high schools but also at the university level. Todd Heywood, a Michigan HIV media activist, has struggled with the safe sex laws in the state for decades. In the early 90s, Lansing Community College tried to throw Heywood out for walking across campus and passing out condoms during an HIV program. "They said I had violated the literature distribution policy," he says. He won the fight with a scolding, and the school promised to have condoms available in the future. "They could not pass out condoms because there might be a legal responsibility for the college if the condoms failed. I kid you not that was the reason they were giving. If we're telling kids to protect themselves [like this program did] and this is a way to do it, but we're not giving them the tools, why are we surprised that thirteen- to nineteen-year-olds represent one of the largest segments of newly diagnosed people in the United States?" So, it should not seem irregular then that neither Alex nor Derek was given condoms by their respective sex ed programs. They were each young people in institutions that saw condoms as liabilities, amid pressures from the government and parents to provide inoffensive abstinence-focused education.

By the time Alex graduated high school, he was, as he

says, "completely uninformed about what HIV was." For people in their twenties now, this sentiment is common. Tom Mendivil, age 29, is an HIV education advocate, but he didn't grow up with that awareness: "My experience with HIV/AIDS growing up was honestly kind of not really there. I knew it was a thing. I knew it existed, but I think it's one of those things that you just know it exists. It wasn't something really relevant to me in my life. It was probably one of those things that I was taught in sex ed. But for me I didn't grow up in the 80s." And for others who grew up without the scare of the 80s epidemic, they often just know HIV as "one of those things" taught in sex ed, and that's it.

For Alex Gardner, that was definitely the case. After high school, he experienced a lot of changes. Although he was heterosexual, he did have a one-time experiment with a guy. He realized it wasn't for him. He ended up unemployed shortly after high school, so he decided he would join the Navy. And he was content not ever needing to learn anything more about HIV than what Mott Middle College High School had taught him. Why would he?

The same goes for Derek. He knew about online gay hookup culture, was asked if he was "clean" frequently, and would often reciprocate the question. He moved up to Michigan after high school, and he was sexually active. When asked if he could count the number of sexual partners he's had, he says he used to be able to count on two hands, but no more. All the same, he was not actively seeking to catch anything. He knew how to navigate hookup culture. What else was there to know?

The problem is that HIV, like other STIs, does not

care what your background is. It does not discriminate based on your morality, race, gender, class, sex, sexuality, ethnicity, age, or anything else. There are people who can have sex with a hundred partners and never get it, and there are people who get it during their first time having sex. It does not discriminate. Considering the way each of their sex ed programs were handled in high school, perhaps it is not a major shock.

Alex was infected with HIV on February 12, 2006.

Derek was diagnosed as HIV positive on June 6, 2018.

Both of them were able to tell me the date without having to think about it.

Jake

Down in Tennessee, the story was not all that different. In middle Tennessee, right outside Nashville, a man named Jake Procter spent his high school years learning what it meant to be gay. Compared to Alex, Jake was a lot more sports-oriented. In his spare time, he swam, ran cross-country, and played football. He worked as a lifeguard at the local gym pool, which gave him free access to the rest of the gym. While a part of his motivation was to prep for enlisting in the U.S. Army, another part of him was aiming for an ideal body type. He had consumed enough gay media at the time to know exactly what he wanted to look like, and, as a result, he tried to stay health-conscious. But what did health-conscious mean as a gay male in a Southern high school in the early 2000s?

Like Alex, in school, he was not taught much about HIV. With predominantly abstinence-only education in the rural South, the slide shows and films created by sex ed programs were filled with images of bodies decaying with the labels of different STIs. While HIV was not the most gruesome one by a long shot, educators still taught it as solely the "gay disease," and many considered it a punishment from God for homosexuality. A Public Religion Research Institute survey from 2013 shows that 14% of Americans actively believed that AIDS was "God's punishment for immoral sexual behavior." While that percent is almost half of what it was in 1992, it still speaks to the kinds of stigmas associated with HIV/AIDS. The sex education literature from the 2000s emphasizes the idea that if you have sex, you will get one of these STIs, and if you get one of these STIs, you will be either subhuman or dead.

It is not hard to find any of these presentations from a basic Google search. One PowerPoint from the Southeastern Chapter of the NAACP shows graphic photos of warts, rotting skin, and lesions all over the body. The same presentation goes so far as to connect STIs to bondage, bestiality, and other fetishes, ultimately recommending not to be gay and always practice abstinence. This isn't even a new trend. The first ever sex-ed film, *Damaged Goods* (1914), shows the grotesque effects of what happens when you get syphilis and, as the title suggests, shows how having syphilis makes you "damaged." This film was shown to viewers throughout the U.S. military as required education. From 1996 until 2010, the federal government spent around $1.5 billion dollars on education that was abstinence-only. American sex education has largely been focused on dehumanizing STIs, and these kinds of representation have played a major part in that. That's the kind of messages that Jake received throughout high school. "I didn't know much about HIV except for the normal scare in sex ed. 'Don't have sex, and you'll be fine,'" he says, practically rolling his eyes. When you pair abstinence-only sex education with information about STIs, it is almost always positioned as an obvious effect to breaking abstinence: if you have sex, you get HIV/AIDS; if you wait (in some cases, specifically for marriage), you will "be fine."

And the South is brutally conservative when it comes to sex education. Planned Parenthood says, "7 Southern states [as of summer 2019] either prohibit sex educators from discussing (or even answering questions about) LGBTQ identities and relationships, or actually require sex educators to frame LGBTQ identities and relationships negatively. These laws further stigmatize LGBTQ youth and leave them without the information they need to protect their sexual health, putting them at greater risk for STIs, pregnancy, and unhealthy or abusive relationships." In Jake's school, his entire sexual identity was erased with laws such as these. And in Tennessee's case, the state law forbids any organization that provides abortions from giving sex education to public schools. In places like this, where being gay is not only frowned upon but actively ignored, topics like STIs are not treated seriously, which likely has a hand in this statistic from the Center for Disease Control (CDC): "In 2017, youth aged 13 to 24 made up 21% (8,164) of the 38,739 new HIV diagnoses in the United States and dependent areas. Youth with HIV are the least likely of any age group to be linked to care in a timely manner and have a suppressed viral load. Addressing HIV in youth requires that young people have access to information and tools they need to reduce their risk, make healthy decisions, and get treatment and care if they have HIV." And it should come as little to no surprise that in this age range, 87% of these new diagnoses are young men, and of them, 93% consisted of male-to-male sexual contact. To make matters worse, at least for Jake, the South contributes to around 52% of new HIV diagnoses. And yet most schools, even outside the South, don't offer LGBT resources on sex education, even if it is not explicitly prohibited. This is the kind of world Jake was navigating, with the odds stacked against him and accurate information in short, short supply.

But Jake had more exposure than the limited education offered by his teachers. He also found out about HIV through social rhetoric. During high school, he found that people would treat STIs as the subject of ridicule and shame. "I did hear jokes about it among my classmates," he says, "and when I played my online video games." In many ways, this joking tone mythologized HIV for Jake, showing him that it wasn't something to be taken too seriously, not at the time, as if it only happened to a certain type of person. The jokes did not normalize HIV; they either dismiss it as irrelevant *or* treat it as a phenomenon that happens to inferior people, as if being "STI-free" makes someone superior.

For many, STIs quite often are a joking matter. The website *Jokes4Us* features a page just for STI jokes, with entries such as, "What's the difference between love and herpes? Herpes lasts forever," and "What's green and eats nuts? Gonorrhea." And this is just one of hundreds if not thousands of similar webpages. You can find STI memes, skits, and even comics now. The rhetoric for many of these centers on the idea that STIs are permanent, not caring which ones are curable or treatable. These kinds of jokes subscribe to the notion that people living with STIs are *defined* by their STIs. This creates a specific environment of rhetoric concerning HIV for people: "If you don't have HIV, it's alright to joke about it." While these jokes are probably not held in the utmost esteem, they are considered acceptable for dark humor. Alex Borgella, in his article, "Science Deconstructs Humor," talks about one possible reason for these dark jokes being funny to many, the superiority theory: "It is the oldest of all humor theories: Philosophers such as Aristotle and Plato alluded to the idea behind the superiority theory thousands of years ago. It suggests that all humor is derived from the misfortunes of others– and therefore, our own relative superiority. Thomas Hobbes also alluded to this theory in his book 'Leviathan,' suggesting that humor results in any situation where there's a sudden realization of how much better we are than our direct competition." This theory offers the possibility that HIV jokes are not just about dismissing HIV's reality but also about separating those with HIV as inferior.

The comedy industry has had a complex relationship with HIV especially in recent years. Comedians like Michael Henry, Sampson McCormick, and Tom E. Brown with his film *Pushing Dead*, have all used comedy to actually advocate for HIV awareness and destigmatization, fighting against the darker humor of the Internet. Shawn Dekker writes about his experiences living with HIV in a comedy memoir entitled, *My Pet Virus*, and he jokes about his titular pet throughout, unashamed of any judgment. And since the book's release in the mid-2000s, Dekker has seen wave after wave of positive feedback: "It was such a whirlwind—the first wave was the reviews. It was very heartening to see *My Pet Virus* mentioned favorably in some major publications. But the true test for me was: how would my story resonate with others with HIV?" And, predictably, people living with HIV loved the work Dekker did. Rather than being upset by his often morbid humor, people would share their own stories of living with HIV in response to Dekker's.

This kind of work—comedians who are reappropriating HIV as a still relevant phenomenon, as opposed to this thing that nobody, or at least no decent person, has—is definitely reshaping the way that humor plays into STI discourse, but people who went to high school in the 90s or 2000s are still dealing with an older rhetoric that only allows for STIs to be the butt of the joke. Because of that, HIV was hard to see as a serious issue. Now, the word "serious" gets complex here. It is not that these people thought HIV was not real or that it could not actually ruin lives. It is more that they saw it as an unlikely threat for them. If jokes help to minimize STIs, revealing their hosting bodies as essentially less than human, then clearly, in their minds, HIV could not affect them.

The world Jake grew up in had minimal education about HIV in the public school system of Tennessee, and, outside of school, it was seen as something not worth taking seriously. But despite all of this, Jake *did* get education about HIV when he turned sixteen and joined a local

LGBT youth group. He had just gotten his first car and started driving. While he told his conservative parents he was attending a Wednesday church service, he was actually driving to north Nashville and meeting with a youth group that met from 6 to 9 p.m. That is where he received what he called a "proper LGBT education, both in history and in sexual education." While they did not spend a lot of time talking about STIs, they did stress the importance of both condoms and lube. For Jake, the group was a lifesaver, helping him to come to terms with who he was as a person. "They promoted a safe space for all, and that really made me the person I am today." This group provided most of the foundations for Jake's knowledge of sexual practices and safety, but even it had its limits, especially in regards to STI discourse.

For the LGBT community more largely, STIs were more openly talked about. LGBT resource centers have for decades offered condoms for free and information on safe sex practices without stigmatizing people living with STIs. There have been massive debates in the LGBT community on whether or not we want to call HIV a "gay disease." Originally, in the 80s, it was very much called a gay disease simply because homosexuals were one of the major identified risk groups at the time. Health education's response was to "de-gay" HIV/AIDS, telling people that anyone and everyone could get it. However, in the late 90s and early 2000s, the LGBT community worked to "re-gay" HIV, showing that while, yes, it could affect anyone, it has mostly affected the LGBT community, and that is where most of the activism has appeared for decades. Sarah Schulman, author of 1990 novel *People in Trouble*, critiques the popular musical *RENT*—which took most of its plot from her earlier novel—as "straightwashing" the reality of AIDS in the 80s by making it so "that the white straight man becomes the central character." While the biological virus can attack anyone, the culture around HIV has been predominantly queer, and an awareness of that is essential for shaping cultural ethics around the disease.

In the 2000s, there was still a certain stigma attached to HIV, even in these communities. Even Jake had connected HIV with sexual promiscuity: "I wouldn't take the subject of HIV too serious in my earlier twenties because I was not sleeping around. I had a few serious relationships but only one fling," and even that fling was an encounter Jake hoped would become more serious. And promiscuity has that connotation of being physically and morally unclean. *Urban Dictionary* has an entry of "walking hiv [*sic*]," defined as a "slut" or "whore." Elizabeth Pisani, in her blog *The Wisdom of Whores*, tackles a lot of slut-shaming that happens globally and its frequent connection with STIs, especially HIV. HIV prevention writer Gus Cairns said in the late 2000s that one of the major ways to fight HIV that's often "neglected" is what he and others at the time called "being faithful." With this kind of association, young people can easily assume that the chance of contracting STIs has a 1:1 ratio with the number of sexual partners they have. They often do not harbor the possibility that it is far riskier to have sex with one person unprotected than ten people protected. This is definitely true of Jake.

He was gay, but he managed to live a fairly normal life

in Nashville. In school, he kept up good grades, especially in psychology and social studies, and he had a good social life. "I hung out with almost everybody," he says. And he had your average high school problems, like cars. His first car, when he was a junior, he wrecked within thirty days. After that, he had a truck. It lasted five days before a friend of his rear-ended it. His luck with relationships was not much better. His senior year, he dated a guy. While it wasn't his first time with another man, it was his first major relationship. While Jake was 17, his partner, James, was in his mid-twenties. The relationship became physically and emotionally abusive. After they broke up, James threw all of Jake's stuff out into the streets. Jake got help from friends and worked on moving on. After high school, he joined the U.S. Army and made a life for himself.

This shouldn't be a surprise though. Every year, kids graduate high school with similar knowledge about STIs to (and often less than) Jake's, and they go on about their lives just fine. Only around a third of a percent of the population has HIV. In 2017, there were almost 40,000 new diagnoses in the country. In the grand scheme of things, is that really that many? Well, perhaps what is most terrifying is that almost half of those new diagnoses were AIDS diagnoses. That means that almost half of the people who were told they had contracted HIV found out they had had it for quite a while and likely had no idea. Their immune systems were running at around 15% of what is considered healthy. A lot of these people are leading normal lives without even a suspicion that a virus is inside them.

Jake Procter managed to live a normal life. He had a

career, a social life, and his own hobbies. He had a caring family, and he was still exploring his romantic side. Like Alex and Derek though, not everything worked out the way he planned it.

Jake was diagnosed as HIV positive on June 18th, 2016.

Like Alex and Derek, he didn't have to think about that date. He knew it off the top of his head. No hesitation. "It's the day my career ended," he says. "I'll never forget that."

Clint and George

So far, all the people discussed have grown up in the 90s and 2000s. They only heard about the 80s AIDS epidemic as a historical event (if they heard about it at all), and their sex education was rather limited, especially regarding HIV/AIDS. But what happens when we look at people who actually lived through the 80s, the people who were around when HIV/AIDS was first discovered? What happens when we look at people who, in theory, should have been very aware of HIV/AIDS and see how it affects their relationship to the virus? Does this knowledge help or at least color their awareness of HIV as a serious threat?

Meet Clint Franklin. He was born in the mid-60s in Philadelphia. A gay black man in high school, he was "well aware of STIs, as well as HIV and AIDS," he says. He had seen it everywhere: on the TV, from friends, and in the papers. He was seeing the epidemic decimate the gay population around him. But in high school, both of his parents were teachers, and he attended a small private school, around 250 students from kindergarten to twelfth grade.

Even back then, this school had decent sex education. While he was not out of the closet growing up—and nor did he really discuss his sexuality with his parents—he was aware of his sexuality. Occasionally, he would hear gay jokes or be called a "faggot," but this was not something that particularly bothered him. Because the school was so small, people stuck together. "My school was really diverse, and most kids were from middle-class families so the school didn't put up with much drama," he says. He had a lot of gay friends in his social circles, and this helped to shape much of his sexual awareness. "I was going out to gay bars at a young age," he says, "and was even a member of a gay youth group at one point." And having lived through the 80s, he was more than aware of how serious HIV/AIDS was as a threat to the gay community. He was aware that it could happen to anybody.

Judging by the way this book has organized the previous two sections, I have no doubt you can predict that like Alex, Derek, and Jake, Clint becomes diagnosed with HIV, and you are correct in that assumption. He received the diagnosis when he was in his mid-thirties, in 2000. Like the others, he remembers that year without having to think about it. But instead of focusing on the ways his education shaped his thinking about HIV, it is more interesting to look at the ways it affected his life and relationships and the decisions he made.

He moved around in Philadelphia for several years, hopping from place to place, but then, in 1989, he moved to Chicago. He has lived in Chicago ever since, and it was a major change for him. It was really his first time being on his own. His life in Philadelphia had been so strict and structured, with expectations and responsibilities dogging him the whole time. "Being the only son of two Southern-born school teachers and the father being ex-military," he says, "moving to Chicago allowed me to be truly free." And it helped him be even freer when it came to his sexuality. But not all the structure was bad for him, especially when it came to his educational background.

In many ways, Clint was privileged to have the education he did. Many black people, both in the 80s and today, have not had the same access to comprehensive sex education. In 2017, while blacks comprised 13% of the United States population, they also were 43% of the new HIV diagnoses that year. The Henry J. Kaiser Family Foundation has a fact sheet available on "Black Americans and HIV/AIDS: The Basics," in which they discuss many of the CDC's statistics and findings about the black community's struggles with the virus: "A number of challenges contribute to the epidemic among Blacks, including poverty, lack of access to health care, higher rates of some sexually transmitted infections and smaller sexual networks, lack of awareness of HIV status, and stigma." And these kinds of intersectionalities are important. Todd Heywood speaks to the connections as being worrisome, "The epidemic has really settled into African American men who have sex with men, especially in the South. And we're not doing anything to address either the racial disparities or the sexual orientation disparities. They are interconnected but also really independent of each other in terms of the stigmas." This information has started seeping into areas like HIV case management, too. Fiza Irfan, a case manager at Lansing Area AIDS Network in Michigan, says that one of her major concerns currently is "trying to reach marginalized populations about HIV, education, and prevention." She has noticed over the years the intersectionalities Heywood speaks of, and "a lot of that," she says, "has to do with familial stuff or culture, and if we could just tap into those pockets and communities and just let them know HIV is a thing, [we could help them] get protected, whatever that means for you." And she argues it is not enough to be aware of these intersectionalities, that we should actively target these communities as well: "Nowadays we see it in the media how black people are disproportionately fucked around with in so many aspects of their lives. It's important to at least target the community, as well as the Latinx community and Asian American community." And these overlaps in social issues make these kinds of action particularly difficult. Almost a quarter of the new HIV diagnoses in 2017 were from the Latinx community, mostly from male-to-male sexual contact. Sex education does not largely target these communities, however, especially in America. In gay Chicago in the 90s and 2000s, this incredibly diverse city was full of these kinds of intersectionality. Unfortunately, it also was one of the meccas of HIV. In 2001 alone, it had over 1,850 new diagnoses of HIV. Compare that to 2016 when the city had only 839 diagnoses. In the early 2000s, it was a tough time to be gay in Chicago.

For Clint, he was lucky enough to receive private education and a considerable amount of sex education. By the time he moved to Chicago, he was aware of more safer sex practices than Jake, Derek, and Alex probably were. And, as he entered the gay dating sphere of Chicago, he found love. With someone he considered "the love of [his] life," they were together for almost ten years. Then, the guy left him. Clint was devastated for months and could not return to work for a solid three months. As he struggled to handle the rejection, he found a rebound almost instantly. He was not in a good place to think about what he needed or what he wanted. A big part of him probably just craved escape. And when you enter that mentality, things like safety usually are not at the forefront of your mind.

A new type of rhetoric has entered the scene of sex education. Often, instead of advocating for "safer sex practices," some pedagogical techniques necessitate stating something more along the lines of "reducing risky sex practices." These risky behaviors include multiple partners, not being on PrEP or PEP, visiting sex clubs or bathhouses, and of course bareback (or condomless) sex. Dr. Robert Weiss in his book *Cruise Control: Understanding Sex Addiction in Gay Men* examines the ways that specifically *persistent* seeking of high-risk sexual activity is a major symptom of clinical sex addiction. He manages to make these claims without "slut-shaming" or even "bareback-shaming," focusing in on the behavioral phenomenon that is much more geared toward inflicting self-harm in a trance-like state. Perhaps, this is the kind of trouble Clint was getting into in Chicago with his rebound partner: "It turns out this rebound was an emotional wreck, a liar, and a drug user," he says. "And I was not stable enough to figure that out in time." Sexually, Clint identified as what is called a "top," meaning the sexually penetrative partner, and as numerous statistics have shown, topping poses a lesser threat of contracting HIV than "bottoming." So, when the rebound told Clint he was HIV-positive, Clint thought the risk was negligible. While the risk is indeed much smaller, it still depends on a number of factors, including protection and the HIV-positive person's viral load. But Clint was not concerned with such things, having just gotten out of a major break-up. "I was damaged and careless," he says, "and he infected me." At least with Clint's case, risky behavior led to him contracting HIV, but it is not like he was actively seeking to get it. There had been communication beforehand. They were both educated to a point. What actually went wrong here? What do we do about this?

People are increasingly focused on a rhetoric of blame when it comes to HIV. Who gave it to you? Who caused it? How did this happen? Sex education might be a major part of these answers. For Clint, it could be as simple as education's not focusing on the fact that it can happen to tops, too. But when discussing HIV, things are rarely so simple. How do we as individuals find the need to care about such safe sex practices when we are at our weakest, when we just need somebody to hold for the night, even anybody? Sex education may not be the complete answer, but it is a place to start, a point of departure. And perhaps, the definition needs to be shifted. As we have seen with all of these people so far, sex education is more than just formal education; it is also the cultural standards in vogue that shape people's awareness of HIV.

Ben and Emily

But for all our talk of blame, this chapter so far has only

focused on the repercussions of male-to-male sexual contact. And, whether HIV is a "gay disease" or not, it biologically can affect everyone. In heteronormative culture, it is perhaps even more stigmatized than in the LGBT community, where there are support groups and advocacy meetings for HIV across the country, plus resource centers to discover these kinds of events. For straight people, that opportunity for outreach is much more limited if not absent. If you're straight and you find out you have HIV, where would you even go? What options are there? And while the truth is that there are many, sex education programs do not really prepare you for how actually to find that help. If you are straight, you might be harder pressed to immediately find the network that can get you the resources you need.

Meet Ben Rogers. In many ways, Ben's story is a love story, albeit a tragic one. For years, he had been working as a plumber and occasional electrician in Jackson, Tennessee, a small city almost equidistant from Memphis and Nashville. Jackson is what the surrounding towns and communities call "the city." If someone in Lexington, Tennessee (about thirty minutes away) says they are going to the city for the weekend, they mean Jackson. In 2004, there were 62,435 people living in Jackson. For comparison, Nashville had over 581,000, and Memphis had 680,000. Ben had a fair amount of work in the city, and it paid decently. But after recently getting out of a relationship, he was a 47-year-old single man and hoping to change that single status. So, he became a regular at a few bars. One late night after work, he met someone at a hotel lounge in Jackson. Her name was Emily Morris. She was a

40-year-old bank clerk. Every night, there was a DJ, and there was a hardwood dance floor in the center. Off to the side was a bar with tables and chairs near it. The lights were always dim. The two had seen each other there several times, but this time was different. They started talking, but Ben had already gained a reputation at the bar. "Everybody told me that I did not need to mess around with him," Emily says, thinking back, "because he wasn't good news, and I guess that bad boy persona kind of attracted me to him. He told me things from his life, and I felt sorry for him." They started dating. They had fun times. They went to yard sales and flea markets, watched all the local car races, and hung out with friends. And after three months, they moved into a house together. It was a small one, but it worked for them. They started a routine. But things quickly took a turn for the worse. Over time, Ben started to drink more. He started to show abusive tendencies, emotionally, physically, and sexually. The charm of Ben's bad boy persona quickly wore off. "I regret it now," Emily says. "I wish I'd never done it."

Clearly though, the troubles these two went through are different from what has been happening in the previous chapters. Neither were invested in gay sex clubs or hookup apps or exploring their sexuality. They were not engaging in the same kinds of risk activity, and both of them were unabashedly straight, leaving no room for the "God is giving you AIDS because you're a homosexual" spiel. Despite their troubles, they were fairly "normal." HIV does not care. In 2001, the CDC surveys showed that 15% of newly diagnosed men contracted it from heterosexual intercourse, and 75% of newly diagnosed women contracted it from heterosexual intercourse. Another major cause of HIV is through needle-sharing, something that was responsible for around a fifth of the new diagnoses that year, which affects people of all sexualities. And this does not even speak to the children born with it. Shawn Dekker, too, speaks of hemophilia and living with HIV in his book. There are so many aspects to contracting HIV, and giving it a sexuality, "gay disease" or not—while still the majority of cases coming from homosexual intercourse—leaves out a lot of other people. People still think of it as *solely* a sexually-transmitted infection and therefore, for many, a disease of shame.

For Ben and Emily, the shame was still yet to come. In early 2006, Ben kept getting sick. He could not even shake a cold. He would take basic cold medicines, but they didn't work. They waited months before actually going to see a doctor, and, at that point, they really had no choice. He had become so weak and so tired. He was constantly coughing, and nothing could make him stop. It was terrifying for both of them. When they went to the doctor, they did some bloodwork on him, and they said they would get the results back in a few days, and they would let the couple know.

Even with the occasional frightening image from abstinence-only sex education presentations and films, people do not usually know what HIV *looks* like. People might assume it looks like having lesions, sores, bumps, etc. But they usually do not think it looks like a normal person, and they definitely do not think the early symptoms just look like the flu. So, to start, HIV is a retrovirus. This means that its genetic material is in what's called

RNA *instead of* DNA. So when HIV enters a cell in your body, its RNA is transformed into DNA, and it becomes part of the cell's own DNA. Once it is in the cell, it is hidden until the cell replicates, and then it activates again. This is at least part of what makes killing HIV so hard. The medicine can kill the viruses in your body with no problem. But it can't tackle the infected cells. Unless they're replicating, it is hard to detect. It's a slow but potent virus in this way. So, what the virus tackles is your immune system. Everyone has what are called CD4 cells. At any given moment, the average person has between 500 and 1,500 CD4 cells in a cubic milliliter of blood. When you're sick, you might be closer to 500. When you've been drinking V8 fairly regularly, you might be closer to 1,500. But a lot of that just depends on the individual, too. And HIV *attacks* these CD4 cells. Constantly. When I was diagnosed, I had about 280 left. When you have 200 or fewer, that is what is called AIDS. As HIV spreads and destroys your immune system, your body is in a constant state of inflammation. The smallest and simplest of sicknesses can kill you suddenly, when they were not even considered lethal illnesses to humans before. When Ben was sick with what seemed like a flu, the usual flu medicines did nothing. His CD4 count was dropping even as the medicine tried to do something, anything.

However, people do not always get symptoms as strong as Ben's. They really don't. George Harris, a black gay man from Nashville, Tennessee, had zero sex ed in school. He did not really learn about sex until an MTV program on the subject in the late 90s. But when George got HIV, it was a total shock to him: "I know that it was from unprotected sex," he says. "But I don't know with whom because I had numerous times where I had unprotected sex. Many of them were with people with whom I would have sex multiple times and when I asked each one of them after my diagnosis, they all said they were positive." He was diagnosed in February 2005. He had no symptoms. "When I received my diagnosis, I was classified as having 'full-blown AIDS,' but I showed no signs of illness, and I was completely healthy otherwise." In part, this is why so many LGBT resource centers and medical professionals recommend getting STI tests every six months. Symptoms can be latent or altogether nonexistent. Connecting STIs with some visual image of symptoms might instill fear, but it does not lead to an accurate mental depiction of STIs for the sake of either self-diagnosis or of stigmatizing people who are now living very healthy lives despite having an STI.

One study from the *Healthy Psychology* journal in 2007 showed that fear-based sex education, usually centered on connecting graphic symptoms to the societal image of the disease, is problematic: "Inducing fear is not an effective way to promote HIV-relevant learning or condom use either immediately following the intervention or later on. However, HIV counseling and testing can provide an outlet for HIV-related anxiety and, subsequently, gains in both knowledge and behavior change immediately and longitudinally." Furthermore, the focus on symptoms creates unrealistic expectations for sex safety. As Cody Sigel says, "Showing images of symptomatic genitals might lead some youth to believe that if their own genitals do not look like those shown in the image, they and their partner must not be infected with an STI." For George, that had definitely been the running assumption. For the thousands of people diagnosed every year, most of them do not show any symptoms.

The blood work came back for Ben. Despite his symptoms, he did not have the flu. In July of 2006, he was diagnosed HIV positive.

Diego

HIV is more than many of these statistics have shown though. It of course exists outside America. How does sex education differ regarding HIV internationally? How does the representation of HIV change in other countries? How does that affect people living with HIV? What about people who travel here, or people who travel *from* here? HIV is very much a global issue, and people are often unaware of that. The stigmas are not just widespread; they're also *different* everywhere. Same goes for sex ed, medical care, and even dating life. They are all different across the globe.

Diego Chaves was a young man born and raised in southern Brazil in the 90s. By the time he started his undergraduate career in school, he had already detached quite a bit from his family, and he had even cut some of his ties to his hometown. Increasingly, his politics became more and more left wing and radical. He knew he was gay pretty early and had already had a boyfriend. In school, he was primarily an artist, and his politics very frequently came into play with his artwork.

In Brazil, sex education is affected strongly by religious

messages. Not only is abstinence a factor of this education, but that education is also very explicitly anti-LGBT. As a result, Brazil has one of the highest rates of murder related to sexuality and gender identity, coming up to 343 deaths just in 2016. Perhaps predictably, the countries in the world with limited or no sex education suffer consequences for it. China, for example, has no compulsory sex education, and it is currently in an STI epidemic, with rates continuing to rise, according to Dr. Qi Zhang at Old Dominion University. Despite this though, they are one of the only countries that have vending machines with cheap HIV tests. India, another country without compulsory sex education, has the horrifying statistic of 53 percent of children between the ages of 5 and 12 have experienced sexual abuse. In Uganda, the government has numerous times refused to give out condoms, stating that doing so would encourage promiscuity and abortions. Currently, over a quarter of girls aged 15 to 19 are pregnant or have been pregnant. HIV is not just an American problem. It's a global one. Despite this book's focus on HIV in America, keep in mind the ways that these issues might appear globally. We can and need to be taking steps internationally, not just here.

For Diego, he made his own education largely, much like Jake did. Since he stayed educated about sex and STIs, he did not see HIV as a serious problem. The boyfriend he had for undergraduate had been living with HIV for three years. "Since his viral load was undetectable for the most part of our relationship," Diego says, "we would actually not always have protected sex. I just wouldn't care about that when we were together." With an undetectable viral load, there was virtually no risk of infection, and Diego knew that.

So, what exactly is undetectable? Dr. Peter Gulick, one of the doctors who worked on HIV back in the 80s at the Cleveland Clinic Foundation and continues that work today, says, "Undetectable means that we have ways of measuring HIV in the bloodstream now. Back in the day, if we measured at less than 1000 [copies of the virus in a cubic milliliter of blood], that was undetectable. Then it became less than 500, then less than 400, 100, now we can go down to less than 20. In research labs, they can do down to less than 5." While undetectable does not mean that the virus is gone, it does mean it cannot be detected in the blood. "But there are still reservoirs where the virus hides, like in the lymph nodes and the spleen and the brain. We can't measure those levels, but we know it's there, and when we stop medicine those reservoirs activate the virus again." So what does this mean in terms of sexual activity? There is a current political movement in the HIV community called U=U or undetectable means untransmissible. "For the first time," Dr. Gulick says, "we have studies showing over 3,000 discordant couples—positive person and negative person living together—if that person is undetectable for greater than six months, the chance of transmitting the virus to the negative person is zero." While undetectable, you still have to take the daily medicine, but you cannot transmit the virus. You are healthy. Your CD4 count is good and healthy, too. Dr. Stephen Raffanti at the Vanderbilt Medical School, has also worked on HIV since the 80s. He thinks back to the horror of the epidemic and how far it has come: "I saw my first patient in 1982 while still a medical student. He was a Genovese merchant marine who spent his shore time in San Francisco. It was a shock to see how sick he was since some of my colleagues in retrovirology were beginning to have results of the then experimental blood test for HIV, we were terrified at the possibility of a new epidemic." But now, he notes, with the advent of better medicine, "undetectable means untransmissible," he says, repeating the mantra. The HIV comedy writer Shawn Dekker, when asked what he would add to a second edition of *My Pet Virus*, says, "I'd definitely write a humorous take on U=U. Maybe from the viewpoint of my old friend, the condom, pleading his case and sharing glorious tales of the past in a desperate attempt to stay in my life." Dekker knows that undetectable is really changing what HIV means in intimate relationships, and this knowledge is practically common sense for people who work in the HIV medical field.

Diego knew all this from being with his partner. That was a major part of why they felt comfortable having unprotected sex. The risk for transmission is not 0.0001% chance. It's just *zero*. With this in mind, Diego idolized his partner. "My boyfriend was really beautiful, and so maybe I even fetishized it a bit," he says. He speaks to the ways that, even with his knowledge of HIV, it was something that "populated the imaginary" for him. By this, he does not mean that he did not take HIV seriously. Rather, he's suggesting, due to his knowledge of what undetectable means, HIV was more of a fantasy scenario with his partner.

HIV fetishization, while it exists, is very much a *fringe*

activity. Most people who have HIV do not participate in
what is called "bug-chasing" or "gifting" culture. In 2003,
though, *Rolling Stone* featured a cover story called "'Bug
Chasers': The Men Who Long to be HIV+." This piece by
Gregory A. Freeman follows the lives of gift givers—people
who get sexually aroused by the prospect of infecting others—and bug chasers—people who get aroused by the prospect of being infected. At one point, Freeman even provides a statistic: "Cabaj estimates that at least twenty-five
percent of all newly infected gay men" were involved in
the community of bug chasers and gift givers. The whole
article works to show how large this "community" is.
However, in *Newsweek's* follow-up story a month later, "Is
Rolling Stones' HIV Story Wildly Exaggerated?" voices
like Dr. Cabaj's claim that *Rolling Stone* literally fabricat-
ed those statistics, trying to make this very fringe group
seem like dominant queer culture: "Neither Forstein nor
Cabaj [the two medical professionals cited in *Rolling
Stones'* article] had read the article before being contacted
by *Newsweek*. Both men said they are concerned that media attention about the inflated numbers—the article was
hyped on the Drudge Report on Tuesday, and Freeman
appeared on a Fox News program last night to discuss the
piece—will only serve to draw attention away from a very
real public-health problem." *Newsweek* goes on to show
how, while HIV has many real issues, even back in 2003,
this fringe fetish community is not one of the major ones.
And, often the people who *do* engage in this "culture" do
it more as fantasy play, targeting undetectable individuals,
fully aware that they cannot actually contract HIV from
them. Perhaps, this is at least part of what Diego was en-

gaging in, a fetishization of a fantasy, a biological bond that he and his partner would share, even if it was something that could not actually happen. Many might find Diego's claim hard to believe: "How can you just forget that your partner has HIV? How does that 'enter the imaginary?'" Well, since his partner was undetectable, that means he was for all intents and purposes healthy. No physical symptoms. No different behaviors. The only difference was really that he had to take a pill a day and see the doctor every few months. It is easy to forget that the virus is a real thing inside your blood when you're undetectable. HIV was never a negative factor in Diego's relationship with his partner, and they loved each other.

But eventually Diego broke up with his partner. He saw other guys for years, but for two years he was single. It was during this two-year period when he was diagnosed, in January 2016. Of course, the doctor could not tell him who gave him HIV, but even Diego is confident he got it from one of his other partners, not his initial one, during the two years. But perhaps most surprisingly, out of all the people living with HIV in this book, he is one of the only people who could not remember the exact date of his diagnosis.

Perhaps, this is because medication is not as expensive down in Brazil, and the stigma could be less severe. Perhaps, it is simply because Diego had better sex education than most Americans. Ultimately though, the background Diego had regarding HIV shaped him to be in a much better place than many Americans when he was eventually diagnosed. Sex education is far from the only thing that affects HIV culture, but it is still a shaping force. It alters the way people discriminate against people living with HIV, it affects the transmission rates, and it can motivate many who are recently diagnosed to kill themselves. One study has shown that around 13% of people living with HIV have attempted suicide since diagnosis. These people are taught that HIV is a joking matter, like Jake had been; only a gay disease, like Ben had been; something that only happens to certain kinds of people, like Clint had been; or something that is basically invisible from one's life, as Alex had been. Sex education is not *the* root of all problems regarding HIV, but it's *a* root. So perhaps, I hope, it is fitting that we turn from sex education to diagnosis, to see the next stage of HIV culture. After all, it is the next chapter of all of these people's stories. It's the next chapter of their lives. And diagnosis becomes a story of its own.

2 / *Diagnosis*

Alex and Derek

Diagnosis is not as simple as one might think it is. The ways people find out they are HIV-positive can often be cold and dismissive. A lot of the places that can diagnose are not actually equipped to provide resources or even medications. While the actual moment of diagnosis can last just a couple of seconds—a quick visual scan over a piece of paper or hearing those words from a nurse's lips— the aftershocks of diagnosis are crippling for many people, making it little surprise that most of the suicide cases occur within the first year of diagnosis. So, though you are already aware that each of these people was diagnosed with HIV, they all dealt with different aspects of HIV diagnosis and those aftershocks.

There are three common ways that people learn they likely have HIV. The first is from a sexual partner who is discovered to be HIV positive. It is stunning to me even as a reporter the number of interviews I conducted where the person living with HIV said they contracted it from a partner who had actively lied about their status. While I ask you to reserve judgment on those people till the end of the book, realizing that for a lot of people discovery of having HIV is often linked to other factors, like a cheating or lying partner, helps to understand that diagnosis is not often expected. The second way people often learn about their status is through regular STI testing, as most doctors recommend getting tests every six months. The final common way is when people who are in the AIDS stage and do not know it become terribly sick

Currently, there are two major tests for HIV: oral and blood. Oral tests like Oraquick are obtainable at general stores like Wal-Mart for around fifty dollars, and they are what a lot of the rapid tests consist of at LGBT festivals and conferences. The oral test takes about twenty minutes to develop and is fairly easy to administer yourself. The blood test can take a week or two for you to hear results back, although it is more accurate. The usual policy is for the medical facility to call you and inform you if you are negative or call you back in if they have results that are not as hopeful. In person, they have a medical professional sit you down and inform you of your status, and they may or may not hand you a brochure about HIV at that point.

And at least with Americans, most remember the exact date of either diagnosis or infection. It's called your diagnosis day, HIV anniversary, or "pozaversary." Some people are able to remember the exact time of day, too. For Alex Gardner, infected February 12, 2006, he hates that memory. "It's kinda fucked up that I can put an actual date on it," he says. But this had been a crippling moment for a number of reasons for Alex. "I believe it was about September of that year when I was still unemployed and decided I was going to join the Navy." He ended up going through with it. He went through the entire enlisting procedure, and, of course, they ran a physical plus blood work. "They called me two weeks later, telling me they needed me to come back to the center." He had no way of predicting what came next. "I was informed that I was HIV-positive and was barred from enlisting in the military...for life. It didn't really sink in until I got back home and the recruiter drove away when I realized what had happened." With his nonexistent sex education, he had no basis to judge what his condition was.

He told his stepfather and grandmother about it immediately, and, within the first thirty minutes of him getting home, he called the one guy he had and has ever had sex with. "It had to be him because it was my first and at that time only time having sex before getting diagnosed." The guy denied everything and claimed that Alex "must be a slut."

Derek Williams' story is not too different. He had gotten strong flu-like symptoms as well as antibiotic-resistant pneumonia in the summer of 2018, and doctors told him he likely had the virus for about eight and a half years. "Prior to diagnosis," he says, "my primary care doctor was following up with my visits due to the pneumonia and filled a few blood tests, with HIV being one of them due to myself being severely underweight." According to the tests run at Mercy Health Hospital, he had well over 800,000 copies of the virus in a cubic milliliter of blood. For comparison, undetectable means less than 200 copies, and AIDSMap calls over 100,000 high. During his stay at Spectrum Health "Butterworth" Grand Rapids Hospital for the pneumonia treatment, he was given a referral to a

clinic and some resource books, as well as being asked if he
wanted to join a support group. But when he looks back
on his experience, he considers it typical. He says his story
is just another "simple case of 'a partner had it who said
they were clean, but was actually lying about their status.'"

There is this trope in HIV narratives that can be called
the "AIDS monster" or in some cases "HIV avenger." The
idea came up originally through Randy Shilts' exposé of
HIV in the 80s, *And the Band Played On.* In the book, he
follows the narrative of Gaetan Dugas, whom he calls "Patient Zero," someone who supposedly intentionally went
around and deliberately infected countless people with
HIV: "At the center of the cluster diagram [of the early
HIV cases] was Gaetan Dugas, marked on the chart as Patient Zero of the GRID [Gay-Related Immunodeficiency
Disease] epidemic. His role truly was remarkable. At least
40 of the first 248 gay men diagnosed with GRID in the
United States, as of April 12, 1982, either had had sex with
Gaetan Dugas or had had sex with someone who had."
Shilts goes on to outline some of the branches of this diagram: "The links sometimes were extended for many gen-
erations of sexual contacts, giving frightening insight into
how rapidly the epidemic had spread before anyone knew
about it. Before one of Gaetan's Los Angeles boyfriends
came down with *Pneumocystis*, for example, he had had
sex with another Angelino who came down with Kaposi's
sarcoma and with a Florida man who contracted both Kaposi's and the pneumonia. The Los Angeles contact, in
turn, cavorted with two other Los Angeles men who later
came down with Kaposi's, one of whom infected still another southern California man who was suffering from

KS. The Floridian, meanwhile, had sex with a Texan who got Kaposi's sarcoma, a second Florida man who got *Pneumocystis*, and two Georgia men, one of whom got *Pneumocystis* and another who soon found the skin lesions of KS. Before finding these lesions, however, the Georgian had sex with a Pennsylvania man who later came down with both *Pneumocystis* and KS." While this seems fairly objective, Shilts also specifically demonizes Dugas with his prose: "Back in the bathhouse, when the moaning stopped, the young man rolled over on his back for a cigarette. Gaetan Dugas reached up for the lights, turning up the rheostat slowly so his partner's eyes would have time to adjust. He then made a point of eyeing the purple lesions on his chest. 'Gay cancer,' he said, almost as if he were talking to himself. 'Maybe you'll get it too.'" For Shilts, the AIDS monster is Gaetan Dugas. Even if we assume that half the rumors Shilts collected on Dugas are accurate, it is a far stretch to make Dugas the prototypical HIV/AIDS victim. Yet, many do it.

The United Kingdom's press *The Sun* had an article in 2011 titled, "HIV Monster," detailing how a man had infected at least one woman without disclosing his status to her. *DailyMail*'s article had a similar title: "Monster who infected woman with HIV virus and had unprotected sex with seven others is jailed." Edwin Bernard, long-time HIV activist and writer for *POZ Magazine*, says in response to the tabloids: "I have a great deal of compassion for the complainant, who also admits in the BBC interview that she knew nothing about HIV (including, obviously, how to protect herself) before she discovered from Mr. Mabanda's fiancée that she was at risk. But there appears to be no

attempt to understand how or why Mr. Mabanda acquired
HIV himself; continued to have multiple concurrent relationships; and felt unable or unwilling to either use a condom or disclose to most of the women he encountered.
(Interestingly, though, he had disclosed to two of the ten
women.)" He finds that the only sentiment he has agreed
with was one he found on Twitter by KrystleLai, "This
man needs #mentalhealth services not deportation." But
the headlines speak for themselves: people associate HIV
with this kind of intentional infecting, which feeds into
the myths that HIV only happens to certain types of people, as if HIV is associated with immorality. And even in
the cases where intentional infection is on the table, the
conversation turns to criminalization as opposed to mental health.

Todd Heywood, Michigan reporter on HIV, rolls his
eyes at a lot of the AIDS monster tropes. "Part of the
problem," he says, "is the innocent victim thing that
played out in *And the Band Played On*. 'People who had
sex with Gaetan Dugas were innocent victims. He was a
predator. He was a monster.' We still live with that AIDS
monster mythology, that perception that people with HIV
are sneaking around trying to infect everyone. Even as a
person who was not HIV-positive but was in a relationship with someone who was, there was this perception
that David [Todd's partner in the early 90s] was going
around spreading it, and he wasn't. He wasn't really interested in sex." And these are concerns that happen for a lot
of people living with HIV. They are often questioned rig-
orously by family and friends, "Who infected you? Who
did this to you?" Todd sees sex, even with people living

with HIV, a lot more liberally. "The AIDS monstering is still there, and it's a convenient way to not accept responsibility. Unless you're being sexually assaulted, it takes two to tango. If you consented and end up with HIV, you have *some* responsibility, even if somebody knew and lied, but you chose to have sex without a condom, *you made a choice.* Where is *your* responsibility and culpability? We don't have that conversation in our culture."

Fiza Irfan, case manager at Lansing Area AIDS Network in Michigan, takes issue with a lot of the stigmatization and criminalization around HIV, and she has encountered the AIDS monster trope appearing a lot regarding disclosure laws. "It's not fair to individuals living with HIV that they have to serve the penalty for disclosing to a partner. It's different if the person is *trying* to spread the disease, but that rarely happens. Most people aren't malicious. I have heard stories from other individuals in the agency of people being beaten, assaulted, or even killed for disclosing...People get themselves in these dangerous situations. They get themselves killed for that disclosure. They're put in jail if they're not killed, and they might be the healthiest individual you meet. But if you meet the wrong partner, it's the end for you. And we don't have the same laws for herpes or other chronic STIs."

So, we start to see how the AIDS monster started as this specific Patient Zero, Gaetan Dugas, and became a media scapegoat for *all* people living with HIV, and even for newly diagnosed people becomes a code for the people who infected them, either for themselves or for their friends and family. This trope appears in the lives of other people in this chapter, and what makes the image most disturbing perhaps is not only how these people are asked whom to blame but also how these people are labeled AIDS monsters themselves, by people online, friends, and even family. For many, being HIV-positive is not just an indicator of being subhuman; it's an indicator of being somehow *monstrous.*

But despite how shitty all of this sounds, Alex Gardner says of his diagnosis, "This is the start of the dark part of my life living with HIV." As with many people living with HIV, diagnosis is only the beginning.

Jake

Down in Nashville, TN, Jake Procter was a gay military man now. "I was dating an older gentleman for a solid year and hadn't done anything with anyone before him for two years. I would get regular testing due to my employer being a government agency." That year, Jake was renewing his contract and working on completing a five-year plan. Like Alex, he had just gone through a physical and blood work. Then, he received an official letter asking him to come in to the office. He remembers that day vividly. "It was a beautiful June Friday morning. The sun was shining, and the pavement was hot. I enjoy summer with my whole being and felt that I was going to just have to retest due to having a few beers the night before with my Dad to celebrate." But when he walked in, the doctors of the facility and the facility's commander were there, too. The lights were off, since the sun was shining into the room. "The doctors sat on one side of the table, and the commander sat at the head after he told me to take a seat across from the doctors. They slid a manila folder across this large oak table. I opened it." What he was staring at was a brochure, entitled, "What to do when you're HIV positive." "They didn't even say the fucking words to me," Jake says. The doctors and commander knew this was the end of Jake's career in the agency.

"When I was told, I felt a feeling in my very core that I never felt before. I felt as though the world stopped and came to a halt in that moment. I began to get very ill and utilized the trash can that was in this conference room." After the commander asked the doctors to leave, Jake's contract manager was called in. The contract manager tried to comfort Jake, to tell him it wasn't the end of his life, but everything just fell apart for him. "Everything I built, my whole being and person I worked to be, was rubble before my feet."

This story is far from new. The military has long had a policy of banning people who are HIV-positive. Section 5-3-c of the U.S. Department of Defense's *Identification, Surveillance, and Administration of Personnel Infected with Human Immunodeficiency Virus* states, "Applicants for accession who have no military status of any kind at the time of testing and who are confirmed HIV infected will not be enlisted or appointed in any component of the Army." The document goes on to list out the assignment limitations for active duty soldiers who are discovered to be HIV positive: they cannot travel overseas, and they cannot participate in any education programs. Some of this policy is being put into question: the Navy, for example, is starting to allow *some* sailors living with HIV to travel to *some* locations. Due to many of these restrictions,

service members living with HIV have had their liveli-
hoods threatened frequently. In October 2018, Defense
Secretary Jim Mattis pushed a policy called "Deploy or
Get Out!" which would discharge service members who
are unable to be deployed for over twelve months. People
living with HIV therefore would be in this group. Sgt.
Nick Harrison filed a lawsuit against Mattis, and Lambda
Legal helped out with the suit, saying, "Soldiers, sailors,
fighter pilots and marines are seeing their promising ca-
reers cut short, their dreams of service shattered and their
health jeopardized due to antiquated notions about HIV
and the stigma that results....This must end. If the court
doesn't intervene, the Trump administration will continue
to discharge more promising service members living with
HIV, denying them the ability to continue serving their
country. Every day, people living with HIV are suffering
professional setbacks and losing out on career advance-
ment opportunities, and we are asking this court to put an
end to these harmful actions." While the military still has
these outdated stigmas from the 90s, it seems it will be
increasingly difficult for people living with HIV to actively serve in the military.

When Jake learned of his status and his lack of a future
with the military, he had no idea what to do or who to
call. He eventually called his best friend, Sarah. She already had a friend who was HIV-positive, so, at that time,
she had more knowledge than he did. She took the news
hard, but she was there for him. "She helped me pick up
that rubble and put it back together," he says. "She told me
to go home, and she would meet me there." As they
planned to go to a local HIV service agency, Jake decided

to tell his parents before they left, so that they would know what was happening. While they took the news well, "they just asked who," Jake says. They wanted to know who had infected their son. Jake wouldn't give any names.

Jake and Sarah went to the service agency, and they got him set up with what is called the Ryan White HIV/AIDS Program. The program was named after a thirteen-year-old boy who received a blood transfusion in 1984 and contracted HIV from it. Due to prevalent stigmas at the time, the high school tried to deny him access to education, and his mother had to take the case to court. While they won his right to still attend school, he constantly faced discrimination and stigma for his disease. His mom said, "It was really bad. People were really cruel, people said that he had to be gay, that he had to have done something bad or wrong, or he wouldn't have had it. It was God's punishment, we heard the God's punishment a lot. That somehow, some way he had done something he shouldn't have done or he wouldn't have gotten AIDS." And just a month before Ryan was to graduate high school, and a few months before Congress would enact the Ryan White HIV/AIDS Program, he died. "Well a lot of people will say, "Your son was such a hero" and all that, but to me, he was my son. And you know, sometimes it's so confusing, because he was my little boy, and to share him with everybody, because he wasn't perfect, but at the same time, he was my son." For people living with HIV today, though, Ryan White's name is essential to living. Currently, more than half a million people each year receive aid from Ryan White to provide financial assistance for insurance and coverage for HIV medications. As most insurances don't cover those medications, some of which can cost over $3,500 a month, Ryan White takes care of all that. It is literally a life-saving program for over half of the people living with HIV in America today. Without it, even people like Jake might not still be around.

Later that evening, Jake and Sarah ended up in a Wal-Mart parking lot, paying the fifty dollars for the home test. He took the test in the car. "When I saw the test line begin to become reactive, I began to lose it. I broke down again. But this time much more violently." Sarah took him home and eventually felt comfortable leaving him by himself, worried that he would try to kill himself. One study from 2003 showed that, "More than 1 in 3 people infected with HIV in the United States has major depressive disorder, according to analysis of a national probability sample of people in care." This, in turn, increases the suicide rate for people living with HIV. Sarah's concerns for Jake were completely valid, and Dr. Stephen Raffanti at Vanderbilt University agrees: "There are different ways that people respond to being diagnosed with HIV. Most patients need time to digest the idea of having HIV and dealing with its effect on their health and intimate life." To make matters worse, many of the HIV medications have the side effect of increasing depressive and suicidal thoughts. Dr. Pim Brouwers, who works with the National Institute of Mental Health as deputy director for the Institute's HIV department, wrote an article entitled, "Risk of Suicidal Behavior with Use of Efavirenz," published in *Clinical Infection Diseases.* "If you read the article," Dr. Brouwers says, "you can see that potentially the efavirenz increased the risk of people that already have suicidal ideation. The suicide rate of people living with HIV is higher than the standard population. There is a concern certainly there. We look at new medication that is rolled out to make sure that there aren't certain mental health side effects." Two of the major HIV medications that use efavirenz are Sustiva and Atripla. While some HIV specialist clinics like the Vanderbilt Comprehensive Care Center run a full "panel" on patients, including mental health history, to decide what drug to put patients on, most doctors do not. Jake would later be put on a medication containing efavirenz.

When Jake got home, he tried calling his different exes and demanded answers. "The last one I was with would swear up and down it wasn't him. He was already seeing someone else and didn't care much about me anymore. I didn't press him after he sent me a picture of a negative test. He would send me into a downward spiral." He took some time off from his other jobs and stayed with his parents for a while. He helped his mother who was going through surgery and spent time with Sarah most days. Drinking became the way he coped with his new life. "A beer in the shower began to become a normal thing for the next few weeks," and he would drink both morning and night.

He eventually returned to his newer home in Kentucky and continued working there. "I had my rent paid through the summer, so I would need to begin working to get my next check to pay the landlord for my five hundred or so square feet of my personal sanctuary," he says. He cut back on the drinking so that he was sober in the mornings for work. He replaced this habit with smoking. "I needed a vice of some kind," he says, "to just deal with the daily." As college started back for him, he realized he needed to return to some kind of routine. "I got a new motorcycle and just rode from sun-up to sun-down. I ate on the road and explored areas I had never been before. I always tried to cross state lines at least once a day. That motorcycle became an extension of myself. I had ridden them before my diagnosis, but this time became very special to me. It was time for me to just digest and be one with the world." His new lifestyle quickly turned him reclusive, though. "I prided myself on having a somewhat 'outlaw' mentality. I enjoyed being among people without actually interacting with them. I would eat alone at random small town lunch counters and keep to myself. I grew a beard and just began to close my circle. I would be friendly with those who would talk to me, like coworkers, but I would be sure not to show my emotions to them." The only people who got to see the real Jake were Sarah and his mom. But the repetition was still good for him. He finished school and met the person he's still dating today.

Jake's experience dealing with his diagnosis can be read in many different ways. Maybe he was trying to pretend his life hadn't changed. Maybe he was trying to fight it, to live life beyond HIV. Or perhaps he was trying to ride away from it, into a sunset where HIV can't reach him. Regardless, he dealt with it in his own way, and he made sure to have a support system there for him when he needed it. Like Alex, his diagnosis was more complex than just an out-of-the-blue medical condition. It came with strings attached, both to his professional and personal life, and it crushed his dreams. But unlike Alex, he did not have a clear AIDS monster to blame. And in many HIV narratives, there often isn't just an absence of villain; there's also an absence of a hero. No one can come in and save these people except themselves. And so, Jake had to start to pull himself from the rubble.

Clint and George

In the late 90s and early 2000s, Clint Franklin was getting tested fairly regularly at Chicago's public health department. But one day, when he called, expecting the usual negative results, they told him they needed to retest the blood, and it would take another few days. "I was a little nervous," he says, "but coming from such a responsible family, I thought, 'No, not me, that only happens to *other* people.'" The health department called him back, and they gave him the bad news and hung up. Like countless others, his first call was to the likely "source." "I called the guy who infected me, and he was supportive as much as he could." The guy who had infected him was trying to process his own situation, dealing with his own positive status. He was one of only three people that Clint has ever really talked to about his HIV, except his doctor. "I called my doctor who was gay, and he provided me with probably the only mental health support I've had with HIV. I think I've handled it well, but my doctor got me on meds and taught me things I needed to know about HIV."

People rarely think that HIV could have any connection to mental health. Even if they can acknowledge the possibility of higher suicide rates or even higher depression rates, they cannot see how HIV is linked to mental

health. In the United States, the two major health organizations are the Center for Disease Control (CDC) and the
National Institutes of Health (NIH). One of the divisions
of the NIH is called the National Institute of Mental
Health, and in this institute there is a specialized department called the Division of AIDS Research, or DAR. And
this division is altogether separate from the National Institute of Allergy and Infectious Diseases (NIAID). Dr.
Pim Brouwers, deputy director of DAR, just across the
hall from the NIAID offices, speaks to why this division
exists: "There's a large mental health component of HIV. A
lot of people with HIV have issues with depression, anxiety, and more either already prior to acquiring HIV or af-
terwards. There are still substantial neurological problems
with either the disease or potential toxicity from some of
the antivirals. There's a behavioral component: psychoso-
cial factors that affect HIV, particularly issues around behavior change as well as issues around adherence to medication, as well as the whole HIV cascades [also known as
the HIV care continuum] of trying to make sure people
don't get lost in the cascades. We are trying to make sure
that people at risk get tested, and if they test positive, they
get at least two optimal treatments, and people who test
negative but take negative risk factors can take PrEP to
limit their acquiring HIV." PrEP stands for pre-exposure
prophylaxis, a medication similar to the antivirals people
living with HIV take, but it's designed to stop HIV-
negative people from contracting it. Increasingly, PrEP is
made more available, but they are still costly. Goals like
Brouwers' of making PrEP more available to people is
heavily tied to questions of economics (more in the follow-

ing chapter). Brouwers thinks back to his early work in the clinic. "My best experiences were when we were able to, with the introductory antivirals, really very significantly improve the mental health and cognitive abilities of children, potentially help them go back to school. That was fantastic to see that." His worst experiences, on the other hand, were back before there was treatment. "I was testing people for neurocognitive and other issues, and the testing we would do was tiring to them. It would take too long. We'd see them in the clinic on Wednesday, and we'd say, 'Let's come back next Wednesday.' And they'd pass away from the pneumonia before then." But Brouwers acknowledges that these are just examples of what DAR does. "Within the whole framework of HIV research, [this is] a certain component that I think is quite significant. We have a budget to address these issues."

Many of these concerns hit Clint all at once. When he first went to his doctor, his viral load was high, and his CD4 cells were low, around 250. "Of course, in the beginning, until I educated myself," he says, "I went through all that mental stuff, thinking no one is ever going to love me. Am I gonna have to hide from my parents at the end of my life? Who is going to help me? Are people going to stare at me? All that stuff."

For Todd Heywood, diagnosed around the same time, there was a whole other slew of mental issues, and the AIDS monster haunts his narrative. In July 2007, Heywood came down with pneumonia and then Stevens-Johnson syndrome. "I had blisters every place where there could have been sweat. The blisters would pop and swap off. It was painful and gross. I went to see my doctor, and she said, 'Oh my god, that's a herpes outbreak.'" They ran a full STI panel on Heywood, and the only thing that came back positive was HIV. The diagnosis was July 17th, 2007. At 3pm. "Does that tell you how traumatic it was? I know it down to the minute. It was 3:03 when she read the results." As she read them, Heywood went cold. The next three weeks, he had no real emotional understanding of what was going on, and he felt numb. The next few weeks, he developed panic attacks when people touched him, and he started taking antidepressants. He did his own partner notifications. "I reached out to the two men who I had had sex with since my last negative test. One was negative. The other was positive. He had known it for over a year, but he had been rejected by everybody in Grand Rapids, MI, where he was diagnosed, including his family. It was okay to be queer, but it wasn't okay to be queer with HIV. So, he moved to Lansing with that message. He wasn't in care. He wasn't talking about his HIV status. His viral load after I was diagnosed was a million. I remember telling him that I had tested positive and watching him just crumble. He didn't want to transmit it. I was the first person in Lansing he ever told." But Heywood's social circles were not as sympathetic. "I remember telling my friends, my theatre crew, about it, and they wanted to know who *exactly* he was. They wanted to hunt him down and hurt him." Even as Heywood tried to stop this rhetoric, others tried to convince him to prosecute. "I was like, 'Why? For doing exactly what he was told by other queer people?' There was no intent to harm me. I still would have had sex with him if he had told me he was positive. People did not and still do not understand that idea. They feel like somehow it was all his fault. It takes two to fuck."

George Harris, back in Tennessee, describes the same kind of numbness with his diagnosis. "A week after the testing, I was notified by someone from Nashville CARES that he needed to speak with me to get extra information. I met with him on Middle Tennessee State University campus, and we talked. Upon hearing the news, I was completely devastated." He felt like he had betrayed himself, and he entered a kind of emotional coma. His CD4 count was well below 200. His viral load was well over 100,000. When you have HIV, you enter a new discursive life. You have a hundred new acronyms to learn—names for the virus, different care agencies, and various insurance programs—and a constant awareness of numbers that signify your life: your CD4 count and your viral load, for example. When someone asks me how healthy I am, I immediately assume they're asking how many CD4 cells I have. With numbers as bad as George's were, he was diagnosed with "full-blown AIDS."

You may notice that that phrase has appeared in quotation marks a few times so far. With HIV largely being a discursive world, a large part of stigma comes from mere language. The University of South Florida Health website has a "fact sheet" on language about HIV called, "HIV #LanguageMatters: Using Preferred Language to Address Stigma." It labels words like "clean" and "dirty" to be stigmatizing. One phrase it tackles is "full-blown AIDS." Its recommendation is instead, "There is no medical definition for this phrase—simply use the term AIDS, or Stage 3 HIV." George Harris had the virus called HIV, and it was in stage 3, what is called AIDS.

After his diagnosis, he was distraught, and he remembers the day after, he "walked around like a complete zombie." He recalls hanging out with friends. "They asked me if I was okay, and one of them even jokingly asked if I had AIDS." After hearing that, he refused to torture himself. "I decided to take ownership of my situation and just go through the necessary options for treatment. I made a firm decision to not belittle myself or allow negativity to alter my judgment." Over the next few weeks, he made numerous trips to various health clinics across Nashville. He paid visits to Nashville CARES, the local HIV case management and education organization. He enrolled in the Ryan White program to be able to cover his medications. "I also began seeing someone at the Vanderbilt Comprehensive Care Center and someone at the Vanderbilt HIV Trials, where they would draw blood, and I would receive medication from them." He began taking medication in June of 2005. That September, just three months, he was undetectable. He has stayed undetectable ever since.

Getting care and treatment is essential for anyone living with HIV, but going from diagnosis to care is a tough decision for anyone. Not only do you suddenly have to have this awareness of acronyms and numbers, but you also have to develop a whole new social network comprised of medical professionals, counselors, and case managers that you never thought you would need. In 2014, 49% of people living with HIV were undetectable. Viral suppression treatments are working. But a large portion of those who were not virally suppressed still struggle with getting the care and treatment they need. There are a whole number of factors that affect a person's relationship with care and treatment, from ineligibility for Ryan White and other funding to racial profiling and serophobia in the medical community. While these are concerns mostly for the next chapter, diagnosis marks a sudden transition for people living with HIV, and unfortunately it falls entirely on those people's shoulders to seek out the resources they need to take care of themselves, and they're not always in the best frames of mind to take that plunge.

Dr. Peter Gulick, infectious disease specialist, recalls what it was like working with HIV in the 80s. "I thought I was going to have to live with a psychiatrist because I was so depressed almost every day of my existence. I was a cancer specialist, so I took care of patients with malignancies, but at least I could put those patients into remission, and sometimes you keep them alive for many years. But here was a disease where there's a young individual who was otherwise in the earliest part of their life, and yet you could do nothing for them except maybe just watch them die. You just felt totally, unbelievably helpless." Over time, things on that front got better. "It was still frustrating that there were so many pills and side effects. At the present, my most discouraging moments are when patients have the ability to take the meds, have the ability to get better, have the ability to get over the disease, yet they don't take their medicines. They either skip, stop taking them for some reason, or they go away and come back with AIDS." The most troublesome cases for Dr. Gulick though are the patients who were born with HIV. "Back in the day, about 25% of women that were pregnant delivered an HIV-positive baby. Those individuals ended up having to go on meds at a very early age obviously and continue on. When I took care of those individuals when they became adults, they were very frustrated with their life. They got tired of taking their meds. They were still very young, and many of them stopped their meds because they just said, 'I'm tired of it. I don't want to be taking these pills, taking blood tests.'" Just getting care and staying in care is a terrifying prospect for many people, especially newly diagnosed people. Dr. Gulick remembers a time in the early 2000s when he received a new patient living with HIV. The patient was a young black man, much like George and Clint, and once they shook hands, the young man said, "You're not going to treat me well, are you?" Dr. Gulick frowned and replied, "Why do you say that?" The young man said, "Because I'm black." The man's previous primary care provider for his HIV did not treat him well because of his race. Dr. Gulick gave the man the best care he was able to and made sure he felt welcome. If you're black with HIV, the plunge into getting care can be even tougher.

Emily and Ben

Ben's diagnosis had its own complications. For starters, he was a straight man. In July 2006, when the Madison County Health Department called Ben to come back for test results, they told him to bring someone with him. Ben called Emily, his stepfather, and his mother, and they all went to the doctor's office. But Ben went in by himself. The doctors would not let the family accompany him. When Ben exited the office, he was in a state of shock. "He didn't know what to say. He didn't know what to do," Emily says. "I asked him what was wrong, and he told me he'd tell me later, that he needed to go back to the hospital to get more tests done." They had all the tests done at that point. Ben was still quiet. When his mother tried to press him for information, he got angry with her. He just did not want to talk or deal with it at that moment. When Emily was in the car alone with Ben, he finally told her that he had HIV. "When he told me, I just...felt all kinds of emotions. I was mad. I was angry. I was hurt. I was scared." At this point in the interview, she starts breaking down. "I didn't know what was gonna happen. I didn't know whether I had it or not. So his mom and his stepdad took us home, and we had to go the next day to the health department to see the doctor there and for them to get him started on medicines. He really wouldn't talk a lot that night, and he didn't want me to say anything, especially because I was so mad and angry. I would have said, 'You've got AIDS, and what if you gave it to *me*, and what if I...'" She wasn't able to finish that sentence. When she knew Ben's diagnosis, her mind was populated with all the "what ifs."

When they returned to the health department, they did another test to see how far along the virus was in him, and they told Emily that she would need to come in and be tested, too. "He had had to give the names of the people he had been intimate with. He had to give names, so he had to give them mine." The doctors gave Ben and Emily brochures and pamphlets about the virus, but Ben would not look at them. Emily, on the other hand, sat and read every one of them, terrified. They set her up with an appointment to come in and be tested. "I was still mad, still hurt. Still scared senseless. I didn't know what was going to happen. It was hard for me to work, and I stayed emotional all the time."

Across America, the practice these doctors engaged in is in response to "partner-notification laws." The U.S. Department of Health and Human Services runs the *AIDS.gov* website, and on it they speak a bit about these laws: "Many states and some cities have partner-notification laws—meaning that, if you test positive for HIV, you (or your healthcare provider) may be legally obligated to tell your sex or needle-sharing partner(s). In some states, if you are HIV-positive and don't tell your partner(s), you can be charged with a crime. Some health departments require healthcare providers to report the name of your sex and needle-sharing partner(s) if they know that information—even if you refuse to report that information yourself." Many times, these clinics will have you fill out a form upon diagnosis. The form asks you to fill out the following information for each sexual partner you have had in the past six months (or sometimes, even the past year): name, address, phone number, and sometimes email. It then asks you if you plan to inform those partners yourself. If you say no, many of these facilities have the right, if not the obligation, depending on the state, to inform those people themselves. In most states, they are required to keep you anonymous even in these cases. New York, for example, offers new diagnoses with three options: "These options are: have the counselor from the Health Department's PartNer Assistance Program (PNAP) or Contact Notification Assistance Program

(CNAP in New York City) tell your partners for you without ever revealing your identity; tell your partners with the help of your doctor or a PNAP or CNAP counselor; or tell your partners yourself. If you choose to tell partners yourself, a PNAP/CNAP counselor will work with your doctor to confirm that the partner was told. If PNAP/CNAP cannot confirm this, they may also follow-up with you or your partner." For many, disclosure to a partner can be terrifying and outright risky (more to come in chapters 4 and 5). What makes these kinds of laws particularly interesting, however, is that they are almost always HIV-specific. Both partner-notification and disclosure laws usually omit gonorrhea, syphilis, and even chronic STIs like herpes. Even with something like herpes being much less easily treatable than HIV, the law carries specific stigmas toward HIV when it comes to disclosure and partner-notification.

When Emily went to get tested, they did the mouth swab first. "I was waiting for it to come back," she says, "and the doctor that came in was really, really nice." He came back in a little later and said, "Ms. Morris, I don't think you have HIV. So far, it's looking good. You'll still have to take a blood test, and you'll have to come back two more times just to make sure." She sat there, waiting, crying, and scared. She did not have anyone to talk to. She did not have anybody to share her fear with or even her concern for what was going to happen to her. "And all I could think of," she says, "was that I was going to die." The doctor came back later and said, "Ms. Morris, it came back clean. Right now, you do not have HIV. We're going to go on and do the first blood test, and you'll have to come back in." And each time Emily returned to the doctor, the test was negative. "Each time I felt a little bit better and not as scared for myself."

On their way out of the health department, Ben asked her finally, "You're going to leave me now, aren't you?" At first, she did not know what to say. "I was old-fashioned," she says. "I didn't know any of this stuff. It just hit me like a brick wall." For a few minutes, she did not say anything. She didn't know *what* to say. At last, she said she would stay with him, that she wouldn't leave him. They had to go to a different health department for a doctor that could take care of Ben, and they would be responsible for Ben's medications and checking up on his health. "That doctor," Emily recalls, "I really didn't like. I was trying to ask him stuff, and he just told me to keep my mouth shut. I thought that was kinda unfeeling because I had just went through having my life turned upside-down. I was scared and everything, and I was just trying to find things out."

This kind of treatment might seem cold, and typically, even in the medical field, this would generally cause some wide eyes. Dr. Gulick was always taught to treat people the same, for example: "Everybody's a human being with a heart and a soul," he says, "and you treat everyone as a human being. You treat them as good as you would treat yourself or your family. You don't treat them less because they're gay, black, Asian, whatever. I found that the patients with HIV...they were so appreciative of everything you would do for them. They were kind of hesitant, like an animal that had been beaten up and abused for many years, and now somebody was coming in and trying to pull them in because they were afraid. They didn't know if I was going to give them good care. They didn't know if I cared enough for them because of different issues they had had." A former nurse near where Ben was diagnosed, in Dyersburg, TN, Loretta Vaughn Mealer learned about HIV when she was in nursing school in the 90s. Usually, HIV was only talked about in terms of pathiophysiology, but she was also taught about how to act around people living with HIV, despite it being a "kind of scary, 'taboo' subject," she says. "They always instructed us to show the utmost courtesy, professionalism, and compassion toward those patients because they were almost like outcasts actually." Even Dr. Raffanti at Vanderbilt says he treats "people more or less the same," but when he is interacting "with people with HIV, especially new patients, I try to keep in mind the horrible stigma that can be associated with this diagnosis." Yet, while these kinds of standards exist in the medical field, there are always some bad apples, like Ben's doctor.

After the initial doctors' visits, Emily's behavior around Ben started changing. "I was still scared," she says. "I was so scared that I was constantly washing my hands, constantly bleaching stuff, everything I could do." While she knew she was not HIV-positive, she was scared that she did not know everything about how she *could* get it. Even when she gets tested now in the 2010s, she still has the terror that she might have it.

This HIV-flavored germophobia is not uncommon. People interviewed for this book had all kinds of stories that showed this phenomenon: people scared to eat cooking from someone with HIV, people who would put gloves on to shake hands, people who would not share the same bathtub, and people who thought they could get HIV from being in the same room as the person. A major part of this stems from a myth that came about in the 80s: "bodily fluids." Randy Shilts talks about this in *And the Band Played On:* "Nervous health officials and reporters had spent months talking about AIDS being spread through 'bodily fluids.' What they meant to say was semen and blood, but the term 'semen' is one that polite people don't use in conversation, and blood banks still objected to the use of the term 'blood.'" HIV cannot be spread through touch or spit. There was not a specific way that people talked about it back then, though. Just "bodily fluids." The media talked only of those fluids "instead of semen and anal intercourse," Shilts says. Many HIV awareness sites and groups still use the term "bodily fluids" without being more specific, and it helps perpetuate this myth for people that it can be spread through the air, through spit, through kissing, through drinking after one another, etc. But this is a myth that is perpetuated throughout American culture. Without anyone to tell her different, can you really blame Emily? Information was never easily accessible, and in some cases even the medical providers do not offer this information.

Ben and Emily eventually had to come up against the AIDS monster of that narrative. Ben wondered who could have given it to him. Emily confronted him about the one time she had caught him with another woman. "I had come home from work, and he had another lady in the house. I don't know if he had sex with her or not, but he was telling me that he didn't know her name or couldn't have her tested." He had had sex with someone ten years before meeting Emily, and he suspects he contracted HIV from her, but every woman that was tested came back negative, every woman except the one whose name he did not know.

At the doctor's office, Ben was given quite a heavy prescription. He had to take multiple pills, and he had to take them three times a day. Back then, this was called the "cocktail." His life quickly became one of medication, all with varying side effects. Adherence to medication during the cocktail era was hard for many. Nowadays, people only have to take one pill once a day. And pharmacy labs are working to create injectables you would have to take once a month instead. Even since Ben's diagnosis, medicine has come a long way. People living with HIV go to the pharmacy once a month, where their doctor automatically files a refill, and they pick up a bottle of thirty pills. Usually, the person just takes one with a meal in the day, and they don't have to worry about it until the same meal the next day. It is a lot easier than it used to be, and scientists are working to make it even easier.

But, like everything so far, not even medication is ever that simple. For Ben, the side effects made life unbearable, and things constantly declined for him rather than getting better. The medication began adding more problems than it took away.

Diego

Diagnosis is complicated. For many, it immediately becomes an issue of communicating to others first instead of dealing with it yourself first. When Diego Chavez was diagnosed, this was definitely the case. He was diagnosed back in his hometown in Brazil after he had come home from completing his undergraduate degree. At school, he had met a new guy, his current boyfriend. They knew each other for three months before they decided to make their relationship official. They promised to have themselves tested at the local clinic. They wanted to be able to have sex without a condom, to be able to feel that intimacy. And if neither of them had any STIs, then they would be able to do that safely. "And then," Diego says, "I found out I was positive, and he wasn't." For a moment, Diego's boyfriend froze at the news, thinking about it and how to deal with it. "It was only a matter of seconds...but I can never forget those seconds."

Diego's boyfriend told him that there was not going to be a problem and things would keep going as they had been. The two have been together for four years now. There are many words for it: a mixed status couple, a serodifferent couple, a serodiscordant couple. They all refer to a couple with one partner being HIV-negative and the other being HIV-positive (undetectable or not). AVERTHIV, an HIV awareness program, has created a fact sheet about serodiscordant couples, and it features sections on getting tested together, ways to prevent transmission, and disclosure. While a lot of this will be covered in chapter 5, it is still important, even this early in the book, to see that a serodiscordant couple can have unprotected sex without any risk to the HIV-negative partner if the HIV-positive partner is undetectable or if the HIV-negative person is on PrEP. Diego's boyfriend is still negative. And he is not a fringe case. This is an overwhelming majority. As stated in the first chapter, if you are undetectable, you cannot spread your HIV.

Diego loves his boyfriend, and his boyfriend made things a lot easier for him after the diagnosis. "Having him around helped me deal with my diagnosis a lot," Diego says. "But the problem right then was my mom." Diego characterizes his mother as a "stalker." The week of his diagnosis, Diego was not feeling well, and his mother found out about that quickly. "I tried to invent excuses for her, but she just went into my social media, my computer, when I wasn't at home." She read his conversations with his friends, and she "created a whole drama" about it. "Instead of focusing on my own assimilation of facts," Diego says, starting to look away, "I had to focus on how to make her be okay with it. That was my main struggle when I was diagnosed."

You are not legally required to disclose your HIV status to anyone in your family, and some people never do tell their family, like Clint. But some, like Diego, really struggle when they do tell their parents. It's a tough "coming out" on its own. Diego was robbed of the ability to disclose to his mother on his own terms, and he had to do it while still processing his diagnosis himself.

While HIV stigma has its differences in Brazil, what Diego went through there should not seem exceptionally odd given the previous stories in this chapter. While diagnosis itself lasts a mere matter of seconds, it is a moment that imprints itself into each of these individuals' minds, and each diagnosis was affected by various complications: loss of job, dreams crushed, the elusive AIDS monster, shame, fear, and, in Diego's case, a prying parent. None of

these people *asked* for HIV. None of them *expected* it. For
many, the question becomes if the person *deserved* it.
Sometimes, people living with HIV ask themselves that
question. But the one thing that is uncontested is that they
contracted it. They got the virus, regardless of cause, and
what matters most is what these people were able to do
with that knowledge.

3 / *Care*

Alex and Derek

In the last chapter, you saw that there are new expectations on a person recently diagnosed with HIV. On the surface, it seems like these new expectations are simple: you have to learn a few new words, meet new people, and start paying closer attention to your health. Take your pills and go to your doctor's appointments. In theory, this should be pretty easy. But as is becoming the theme of this book, living with HIV is always more complicated than it seems. In this chapter, I explore what can universally be called "care." This includes the various systems put in place to help people living with HIV: case management, insurance, medicine, doctors, etc.

Many people do not realize there are medical facilities equipped to handle people living with HIV, and there are places that are not. When Alex started getting care for his HIV, it was at a clinic that was behind on the times. "Early on," he says, "I was at a clinic that set me up with a doctor. I had group therapy for everything going on." He was still adjusting to his diagnosis and the changes that would be asked of him. "I wasn't taking meds as my numbers were still very, very good. And they don't want to start you on meds until you need to take them."

At the time of Alex's getting care, changes were happening in medical care related to HIV. The medication people living with HIV take is often called antiretroviral therapy or ART. This therapy was introduced in 1986, and one of the major topics of debate among health and medical professionals since then was whether it was best for a person to start on ART immediately or when their CD4 count dropped below around 350. A lot of factors shaped this debate, especially in the 2000s: adverse side effects of ART, possible organ damage if not on ART, limited resources, and physician discretion, to name a few. By 2011, it was a majority belief, however, that patients needed to get started as early as possible on ART. Medical professionals were starting to realize that ART could prevent the spread of the virus as well as keep the patient healthy because of the speed with which treated patients attained undetectable levels. When Alex was told he had to wait to get started on medications, he was definitely seeing a clinic that was a bit behind on the times.

He started a new job at Wal-Mart and thought, because he was making more than minimum wage and his food stamps had been cut, that he would be ineligible for treatment. "I stopped going to the doctors since I couldn't exactly afford it out of pocket, and nor could I afford insurance at eight dollars an hour." While it is true that making above minimum wage affects certain insurances, HIV has a loophole: Ryan White. In Ryan White's section B, there is a program called AIDS Drug Assistance Program or ADAP. The program pays for your ART if you are below a certain income level. Many people I have spoken with assumed that this level, as Alex thought, would be at or below minimum wage, but it is actually much higher. In most states, there are three major criteria for ADAP eligibility: proof of status, proof of residency, and income must not exceed 400% of Federal Poverty Level, or FPL. In 2018, the FPL for an individual was $12,140 a year. So, in most states, if you make below $50,000 a year, you are eligible for ADAP. Some states go much higher with that percent. In Michigan, where Alex lives, it is actually 500% of FPL. I informed Alex of this on June 10, 2019. In his thirteen years since diagnosis, he had never been told this. He had not been on regular treatment since diagnosis.

Shortly after starting the job at Wal-Mart, he was forced to move out of his house. He did not do anything about getting treatment for a long time. "I'd say about a year later, I started to read stories about it and what it could do to you. How it will kill you later on, and I got super depressed. Depressed to the point of being suicidal." It was not until 2015 that he would decide to look back into treatment and insurance. He found out he was eligible for Medicaid, and it would cover his treatment. "I started treatment soon after for about a year. Then in 2016, I started a new job at a garage, and my income doubled overnight." Medicaid immediately cut him off due to his income being too high. And due to his living situation, being the only one in the house of two who could pay bills, he was unable to afford insurance. And so his treatment ended.

Derek, too, went the Medicaid route after his diagnosis. That is how he is currently able to afford his medication. But he knows that if that ever falls through, he has ADAP to fall back on. His case manager has made sure he knows that.

So, what exactly is case management? In most major cities and in a lot of smaller ones too, there are HIV/AIDS agencies that specialize in resource handling for people living with HIV. They are usually able to offer free HIV tests. They provide free condoms. They have more brochures than you would ever think necessary. They often have workers who handle early intervention services, or EIS, for people recently diagnosed. EIS workers help to get you to initial appointments, help get you started on meds, and help keep you adherent. They often have group therapy sessions for different HIV topics. They offer a lot of other services, too: monthly food banks, occasional rent and utility assistance, and public transportation vouchers. They work toward making sure your insurance stays active, your ADAP stays active, your pharmacy keeps your refills ready, and you stay healthy.

Reporter Todd Heywood, diagnosed in 2007, called his local case management agency, Lansing Area AIDS Network (LAAN), within days of his diagnosis. He informed them of the diagnosis, and "they immediately brought me into case management," he says. Since he qualified for low-income health insurance there, he was also able to have Ryan White cover his medications. However, he did not start his treatment until much later. Like Alex, he found the idea of early treatment was met with resistance: "At 2007," Todd says, "the recommendation was to not start medication till your CD4 was 350 or less, which was based on a really large study, but the study participants were drug users and alcoholics." The study did not focus on people who were regularly adherent to medication. It instead focused on people who would only take their medications after symptoms started appearing. Todd argued with the doctors. "And it turns out I was right. I'm quite responsible, and I have the right to start drugs when I want to, not based on some study that doesn't even apply to me."

In the mid-2010s, UNAIDS came up with a proposal for ending the AIDS epidemic by 2020. This plan was called "90-90-90." There are three major goals of 90-90-90: "By 2020, 90% of all people living with HIV will know their HIV status. By 2020, 90% of all people with diagnosed HIV infection will receive sustained antiretroviral therapy. By 2020, 90% of all people receiving antiretroviral therapy will have viral suppression." This model has shaped the way many medical professionals of HIV work. Dr. Gulick has summarized the plan and tries to enforce it: "We need 90% of people diagnosed, 90% of people linked to care, and 90% of people staying in care and undetectable. We really need to try to meet those three requirements as quickly and effectively as possible. So, as far as diagnosis, we have to make everyone aware that it's still there, that it's still in certain groups of individuals, especially where you have substance abusers, IV-drug users, ones that come in with sexually transmitted infections." A part of this of course comes down to sex education, but another part of it happens with just public resources. As colleges are increasingly having events where HIV testing is free and encouraged, and doctors are increasingly rec-

ommending regular STI testing, we can see the efforts in
the medical community to diagnose people who don't
know they have HIV. "We really have to diagnose the cases." But that's just the first "90." "Then, you want to prevent new cases from forming, so that's diagnosing and
that's getting them on therapy. U equals U." Frequently,
this is called Treatment-as-Prevention or TasP. Since being undetectable means your HIV is untransmissible, that
medication factors in not only as keeping the person living
with HIV healthy but also as managing the epidemic.
"And to reduce the new cases even more so, PrEP," Dr.
Gulick adds. Pre-exposure prophylaxis manages the epidemic by just stopping people from getting HIV. Most insurances still do not cover it, and it is incredibly expensive
without insurance, but its development and availability
are steps in the right direction. "Then linking to care. We
need to make sure that primary care physicians, ERs,
wherever, get the patients into care quickly. One new con-
cept that's out there now is 'quick starts.' In the old days,
still now even, a patient comes in, they've recently been
diagnosed. Many times, by the time you get them into
care, get their labs, have them see social workers, everything else, it may be a month, even two months before
they even get on the medicines. Many of them, because the
urgency isn't there and they get a little nervous, they dis-
appear. Because they don't see the urgency, they're not doing something, so why would they want to keep coming
in? Now, there's quick starts, meaning within a week,
sometimes several hours, two weeks max, you start the patient on therapy. You get the patient in, make sure they're
positive. Even without all the labs back, you get them on

medicine right away. Then, the patient can feel like there is an urgency. That's a big frustration too: staying in care. I just had a patient who's been out of care since August. He comes in. He goes out. When he goes out, he develops AIDS again. So then, he gets AIDS, all the complications there. Then, he comes back in. And each time that happens, when his T-cells go up and down and his viral load goes up, that causes more serious problems with that patient immunologically. His body won't recover as well each time that happens. We've got to keep them in care, keep them on medicine."

HIV care is a large system as a result. With each of these three stages—diagnosis, link to care, and sustenance of that care—there are countless individuals involved. Dr. Gulick views this as a well-oiled machine: "I'm part of a team to take care of HIV. I'm just one part though. I'm just one cog. We need more cogs in the wheel, including mental health, substance abuse, social service, case management, all to give to that *one patient*, so that we can keep them in care. So that if they've got mental health issues, we can get those mental health issues under control. Get the substance abuse under control. Get their living conditions under control. I'm just one cog. We need all those other cogs. We need all those other people in this village of providers to take care of the HIV patients to keep them in care and keep them on their medicine so they can get suppressed."

When I said at the beginning of this chapter that care is complicated, this is what I mean. When you are diagnosed with HIV, you are suddenly a resident of this village. While they are all there to help you and care for you, it is a whole new social sphere you never thought you would have to navigate, a whole new world. Each person has their own relationship with you, and you might have different expectations from and for each relationship. If this is a well-oiled machine, it is one that you are expected to keep oiled and maintained. Sometimes, like Alex's case, you're not handed a manual for it either. And, as a result, a lot can go wrong with the machine.

Jake

Jake's entrance into care seemed smooth at first. He was already on his parents' insurance, so he did not have to worry about getting signed on to entirely new insurance overnight like many people living with HIV do. His first doctor was not the most aware, however. "He treated me very differently," Jake says. "Like I wasn't a person. The man didn't even shake my fucking hand." That visit lasted only fifteen minutes. The doctor told him what his counts were, but Jake had no idea what they actually meant. "I knew that my viral load was high, and that was bad." The doctor ended up prescribing Atripla for him. At the time, Atripla was infamous for heightening suicidal ideation and depression. When Atripla was around, there were already several other medications that were available that did not have those side effects. Atripla was not the most effective medication by a long shot. *POZ Magazine's* 2018 HIV Drug Chart shows eleven single-pill medications for HIV. Nine of them do not require efavirenz, the depressive element of Atripla (Atripla being one of the two that do require it). But for doctors who do not regularly follow

HIV medications, they stick with what they know and have used in the past. Atripla.

Jake characterizes the side effects as "awful." *RXList* has a list of all the major side effects of Atripla: "dizziness, trouble sleeping, drowsiness, unusual dreams, and trouble concentrating." To make matters worse, doctors frequently recommend taking it at bedtime since it is best taken on an empty stomach. These side effects became daily life for Jake. "Made me tired all the time," Jake says, "gained weight, felt sick a majority of the day and gave me awful nightmares. These nightmares were very real to me."

But Jake was determined not to see this doctor again. Sarah, his best friend, saw him struggling with the medications and explained that he should go to a different provider. Another friend of hers who had been living with HIV went to the Vanderbilt Comprehensive Care Center and was able to recommend it. "I then went to them and experienced better care right away. I was switched on medication to Triumeq and have been on it since. I have tolerated that much better." Jake calls the doctor at CCC the "best of the best." "He took the time to listen to me and took a personal interest in me. He took the time to explain everything that needed to be done and would be done. That doctor made a difference in my life and still does to this day. Because he takes the time."

Part of the reason there are so many drugs available for people living with HIV is to make life as easy as possible. For people who struggle with adherence, a single-pill regimen works better than the old cocktail. For people who don't eat regular meals, Genvoya probably is not the best idea, and for people with depression, Atripla also should not be recommended. Unfortunately though, cost becomes an issue, too. While insurance and ADAP can cover medications, sometimes, insurances lapse, and a person living with HIV has to choose between not taking medicine for a few days, weeks, or months, or paying the money they probably don't have. Genvoya, one of the best medications of early 2019, costs $3,100 a month. The most expensive medication is Symfi, which averages around $4,900. The cheapest medications are Delstrigo, Juluca, Odefsey, Complera, and, predictably, Atripla, going between $2,100 and $2,800 a month.

For Jake, the Ryan White helps a lot. He has to recertify every six months, but this process usually goes smoothly. He has to bring his insurance cards, recent paystubs, proof of address, and the agency usually has his other files on hand, like his proof of diagnosis. But, as a result, he does not have to pay for his meds out of pocket.

Dr. Stephen Raffanti from Vanderbilt thinks these medication costs are outrageous: "The cost of medications in this country is just one of the areas where our costs are much higher than they should be. Profit drives innovation," he says, "so drug development is related to profit generation for the pharmas. A pharma company would not invest in the research to develop the drug if the profit motive were not there. That said, the profits of pretty much all the players in healthcare—pharma, insurance, providers, pharmacy benefits management companies—are huge and continue to grow. So, the calculation is how can innovation be driven without creating a system that is so costly that patients with poor or no insurance cannot get care." Fiza Irfan, from LAAN, agrees. "HIV drugs are ex-

tremely expensive," she says, "if you're uninsured. Being uninsured in this country is a problem. The rates are ridiculous."

So, what do these people mean with these critiques? If we were to give pharmas the benefit of the doubt, wouldn't that mean that the retail cost would be similar to the cost of production? Well, across Europe, South America, Africa, and even parts of Asia, generic drugs are often available for anywhere from $75 to $400 a month. Gilead Sciences, Inc. is well-known for its creation of numerous important medications, including eleven major drugs for HIV (including Atripla, Genvoya, and Stribild), medications for hepatitis C, and drugs for liver disease. It is becoming increasingly infamous as a "monopoly" in these areas. So far in 2019, Gilead has been sued at least twice for unethical practices. One of the suits accused Gilead of making deals with patent-only ingredient-manufacturers, even after the patents were expired, keeping the costs of the medicine exorbitantly high. Before this most recent suit, I reached out to numerous people who work at Gilead to speak about some of their philosophies and goals, but the media department there would not let any of the scientists or workers speak with me, and the media department had no interest in this project themselves. No comment.

Clint and George

Clint's entrance into care was centered largely on therapy. Right after diagnosis, his doctor set him up with counseling, especially considering his depression after his first breakup. But he immediately struggled with the therapy. "It just wasn't for me. I couldn't open up to the therapist. I think I have a jaded attitude toward it. I did around three sessions and stopped going. I was back to that attitude of 'I can handle anything on my own,' which got me in trouble in the first place." But his doctor has been there for him the whole time and has kept him on good meds. He has been undetectable ever since.

George did not need as much help from therapy, but he relied more on case management. "I remember riding the bus to and from various appointments, thinking of how this was a very transformational point in my life. It was sort of a clear defining moment. It had to do with the fact that I didn't want to be identified as sick or helpless." While he does not remember his initial meeting, he knows it was all a blur to him. His case managers were all kind and helpful to him. "The medication has been going well. There were a few instances of problems getting my medication in a timely manner. One incident was when I was without medication for nearly three weeks."

So, how exactly do insurances lapse like this? Dr. Gulick blames it on paperwork and a frequent lack of a strong care network in place. "Insurances are changing. These poor patients! They're on one insurance one day, and then they have to go on another one. And many times, there's a gap in their insurances, and then they're off their medicine for a period of time." These kinds of periods without medications lead to CD4 counts dropping and viral loads rising again. "Those are very much a concern, and many times patients get frustrated, and so that's where you need that team so that then the patient can call their case manager or social worker so that right away they can get the thing under control, not waiting months before something happens." Even while Dr. Gulick's area in Lansing, MI, has the Lansing Area AIDS Network, he still finds patients struggling. "I can see the frustration. I'm very frustrated because they're changing all the time." He also points to the pharmacies as being part of the issue. "I try to get the patients into one of these specialty pharmacies, like the one at our center, and they're 340B, so we get the meds at a reduced amount of money, and then we can give them to the patients, and then the money that 340B makes as a result of getting them at a cheap price but still charging the insurance at a higher price, that money goes back into HIV care. We can hire more medical assistants, we can hire more nurses, we can hire people to give better care to HIV patients, so it all works together. Plus, all these pharmacies are used to these drugs. It's not like going to Wal-Mart or Rite-Aid, where they'll say, 'Well, I've never heard of Biktarvy before, and so we don't have it, and I don't know when we can get it,' and the poor patient is out of their meds for a month." But many patients have to go to the big-name pharmacies, especially since they often have weekend and evening hours while the specialty pharmacies don't. Unfortunately, the kinds of lack of awareness Dr. Gulick describes of the big-name pharmacies are fairly common. People living with HIV often encounter pharmacies who say it will be several days if not weeks before they can stock a specific medication. Some clinics have started doing medication delivery, such as the specialty pharmacy that runs out of the Vanderbilt CCC. They drop the package off at the person's house without

HIV being mentioned anywhere on the package.

Frequently, case managers will help when it comes to lapses. Fiza, at LAAN, has been handling case management for years. After finishing school at Michigan State University, she started volunteering at LAAN as a test counselor, ended up in case management shortly after, and now she is the Tobacco Association Program Coordinator there, helping people living with HIV lessen or quit their tobacco use. She has dealt with a lot of cases over the years, and some of them have been tougher than others, but repeatedly, a trend for her cases comes from larger systems, not just the individual. "One of my most warm and fuzzy stories is a gentleman who was released from prison. He was there for around twelve years, and he was re-entering the 'civilian' world." The man had had a history of substance abuse and was repeatedly back in the system. His parents had passed away, he had lost his home, and he was suffering drug addiction. "He was never difficult to work with. He always had the most positive outlook on life. His goal after coming out of prison was to stay healthy and stay out of trouble." He wanted to get his own car and his own permanent residence. "He did so well, and now he's actually living in Illinois, has a full-time job, is in school, and has a home." Fiza's experience has shown that managing these cases is often not about the HIV aspects: "It's more about the person as a whole. You can't label them because of their disease. It's so much more than that."

But her worst experiences in case management have focused more on systematic injustice and intolerance toward individuals. "One specific individual," she notes, "is chronically homeless and has been since he was eighteen when he was kicked out of his home, contracted HIV, and has been in and out of medical care." He has multiple mental health disorders and has been trying to survive on the streets. "The best part is that he has the best perseverance. Even when he's not at his best, when he's angry or someone's disappointed in him, he is still able to come in and get the help he needs. He wants to survive. He'll take his medication for about a year, and then something will happen that triggers a lack of trust in the medical system. Living under bridges and getting sexually assaulted by individuals who he trusted and wanted to crash at their place but gets taken advantage of....The best part of being a part of this agency is seeing how strong people are and how much they have to give. It's humbling being able to work with individuals like that."

With case management handling situations like these, people who are dealing with substance abuse, sexual assault, and homelessness, it is not hard to see how necessary these kinds of agencies are for people living with HIV. Whether it is something "small" like making sure meds are refilled or something larger like trying to provide housing assistance, case management agencies are an important part of the machine, of the village. A lot is asked of them, yet they do their best to deliver, as Clint and George would attest.

Emily and Ben

For Emily and Ben, case management never came into play. And the "care" they would receive was uninformed at best and shoddy at worst. Obviously, medical care is essential, but just having medical care is not often enough. It becomes patients' rights to demand better quality care, not just care's presence.

After Ben had been taking his HIV cocktail for quite a while, something started happening to his eyes. They both went to one side, and he was unable to see clearly anymore. Eventually, he could not drive, and he had to quit his job. Finally, he was admitted at Jackson General Hospital. The doctors checked him, and they informed the couple that there was something on Ben's brain, in a place where they were unequipped to do surgery. So, they sent him to Vanderbilt Medical Center for the doctors there to look at him. At Vanderbilt, a whole team of doctors worked on him. They started Ben on medicines that shrunk his tumor noticeably, something the doctors confessed to not having seen before. As a result, they brought in other doctors and residents to look at him and see what was going on. "He stayed in the hospital for a long time," Emily says. "They did five or six spinal blocks on him. All kinds of testing." Finally, they figured out what was causing the tumor. "The doctors said that the doctor in Jackson that had put Ben on his medication had started him out at way too strong a dosage. They should have started it at a lower dosage." They were sent home with lower-dosage meds and medicine specifically for the tumor.

Over time, the doctors noticed the tumor had finally stopped growing, but it wasn't shrinking any more since that initial shrinkage. His eyes had not gotten any better either. That's when new problems began emerging. "His feet started swelling really bad, and his stomach swelled really, really big. He went up two pants sizes because of his stomach being so swollen. He got where I would have to help him in and out of the bathtub because he was too weak."

Ben's life had gone through so many changes in such a short time, and he was losing not just his health but his independence. "He was all depressed and everything," Emily says. Then, one day, while Emily was at work, the people who lived across the street from her and Ben called her. Ben had tried to kill himself by slitting his wrists. The neighbors had contacted the landlord to break in so they could get him to the hospital. The doctor there sewed him up and let him come home. But Emily had to clean up when she took him home.

"I had to clean up all of that," she says, referring to the blood on the floor. "I was so scared just touching it. I had four or five gloves on. I had to empty the dishpan and clean up everywhere where he had tried to kill himself."

Eventually, Ben's stomach felt unbearably painful, so they had to make another trip to the hospital. Emily talked to the doctor in the emergency room, and he informed her that Ben's stool had turned black. He was internally bleeding. Emily could not believe it. "I was talking to him, and he was doing fine and everything, and the next day I went back up there, they had him in intensive care, and he was in a coma." It was all a shock to her. His family came to visit until visiting hours. Even after those, the doctors let Emily stay there with him. A nurse came in after a while and told Emily that she should go home and rest and that the staff would call her if anything changed.

About six hours later, the nurse called. Ben had taken a

turn for the worse, and Emily needed to call the family to come back up to the hospital. "He lasted for about four hours," Emily says, "and sometimes you could tell that he could hear you because he would squeeze your hand when you asked him something, but then he just quit breathing and passed away."

The blame game quickly becomes complex when it comes to Ben's death. Do we blame the initial clinic that gave Ben an incorrect dosage for his HIV? Do we blame Vanderbilt for not being able to get rid of the tumor? Do we blame the cocktail for increasing his suicidal ideation? Do we blame the "village" for not taking him in? Regardless of whom we blame, Ben died. It was long, drawn-out, and full of medical visits, paperwork, and pills. He did not have the support system that many people living with HIV do, and he lived in a place that did not really have a space to actively take care of him. But Ben and Emily's story shows that, even with medications now able to get people undetectable within a month or two, not everyone is getting sufficient care to get them to that place. Sometimes, that insufficient care is coming from the medical sphere, too. Whether this insufficient care stems from doctors who do not care to connect recently diagnosed patients with resource centers or from medical professionals who do not stay up to date on HIV studies, there are clear lapses in care at the point of treatment.

Many of the people interviewed for this book spoke of prejudices they have seen in the medical world, people who treated them as if their very existence was a biohazard. Todd Heywood was one such person. In 2012, he stepped on a drinking glass. It shattered and sliced into the bottom of his foot. "A friend came and got me and took me to the 'ready' care," he says, "and I went in, and I'm just gushing blood from the bottom of my foot." When a nurse practitioner came in to inform him that he would need stitches, he let her know that he was HIV-positive. She said she would be right back. "She came back in, head-to-toe in biohazard stuff: three layers of gloves, the face shield, the goggles, the full Tyvek suit, footies, hat." When she finished sewing up his foot, she said, "Phew, sewed you up and didn't even poke myself," almost with a giggle. Then, she informed Todd that he was the first person with HIV she'd ever sewn up. Todd was quick to correct her: "No, I'm the first one that told you that I had HIV that you've ever sewn up." When he asked her if she would dress like that for the "little old lady who's sitting out in the lobby with a cut over her eye," she said, "No, why would I?" Todd's response: "Because she's probably in her sixties, maybe seventies, which means she has a high probability that she has hepatitis B or C, which are significantly more infectious to you."

That wasn't the only time Heywood found medical stigma in Michigan. One weekend, a friend of his had been sexually assaulted and had to go to Sparrow Hospital to get what is a called a SANE (sexual assault nurse examiner) exam. While he was given antibiotics, he was sent to the emergency room when he asked for PEP (post-exposure prophylaxis). The physician there refused to write the prescription "because that was only for healthcare members." The physician brought them a contact sheet for the CDC's PEP hotline, and Heywood talked with a representative there who would communicate with

the doctor and have the situation resolved. Twenty
minutes later, the physician gave Heywood's friend the
prescription without apology. The next day, Heywood
wrote an article about the incident, and Sparrow immediately retaliated. "They called and accused me of setting
Sparrow up, that this was all fake, that the victim was not
a victim of sexual assault despite the fact that the victim
had filed a criminal report, that it was investigated, that it
was determined it was sexual assault. All of that was
there."

Former nurse Loretta Vaughn Mealer from Dyersburg,
TN remembers a time in 1998 when she saw a doctor terrified of a patient with HIV. At the time, she was working
at Pemiscot Memorial Hospital in Hayti, MO. "We had a
lady come through that was pregnant, and she was HIV
positive," she says. "The doctor taking care of this one lady
was scared of getting HIV and would not touch the woman at all." Mealer had to take care of the woman herself,
but she knew more about HIV than the doctor did. "I
touched that woman with my hands on her skin without a
glove. I looked her in her eyes when I spoke to her. I did
not show pity for her. I just wanted to take care of her the
best I could."

Dr. Gulick, too, remembers that not every medical
professional has been as aware as he is. When patients are
comfortable with it, he makes sure to give them a hug rather than shake their hand. He wants his patients to know
he is not afraid to touch them, that he does not see them
as biohazards.

On one hand, any ignorance in the medical field can
seem generally innocent. If they never learned, they never

learned, right? Unfortunately, some of that ignorance has become a matter of health policy as well. In 2017, Georgia state representative Betty Price made some rather controversial statements. It is worth noting, too, that she was married to the secretary of Health and Human Services, Tom Price. And Betty Price was formerly an anesthesiologist herself. At a committee meeting, she said the following to the director of the HIV Epidemiology Section for the Georgia Department of Health: "My thinking sometimes goes in strange directions, but before you proceed if you wouldn't mind commenting on the surveillance of partners, tracking of contacts, that sort of thing. What are we legally able to do, and I don't want to say the 'quarantine' word, but I guess I just said it. Is there an ability, since I would guess that public dollars are expended heavily in prophylaxis and treatment of this condition, so we have a public interest in curtailing the spread. What would you advise or are there any methods legally that we could do that would curtail the spread? ....It's almost frightening the number of people who are living that are potentially carriers, well they are carriers, with the potential to spread, whereas in the past they died more readily and then at that point they are not posing a risk. So we've got a huge population posing a risk if they are not in treatment." Price received a lot of public backlash for these statements, and she has since amended her statements. But it is rather telling that someone so involved in health policy did not have the education to understand why quarantining was an impossible project when it comes to HIV, yet found it completely appropriate to bring up in a policy-making committee. She is an example of larger systematic ignorance.

Discrimination against people living with HIV is not uncommon in the medical profession. Numerous studies have documented it, though it is getting better. One article from the American Medical Association *Journal of Ethics* summarizes one such study, "A 2006 study of specific-service health care professionals in Los Angeles County found HIV discrimination to be prevalent. The researchers surveyed 131 skilled nursing facilities, 102 obstetricians, and 98 plastic and cosmetic surgeons to determine how many of these institutions practice a policy of blanket discrimination against people living with HIV. Of the institutions surveyed, 56 percent of the skilled nursing facilities, 47 percent of the obstetricians, and 26 percent of the plastic and cosmetic surgeons refused to treat people living with HIV and had no lawful explanation for their discriminatory policy." While this is over a decade ago, many of the anecdotes in this chapter alone show that that discrimination has not completely gone away, not by a long shot. If people living with HIV need this "village" in order to stay healthy, they need competent and educated people in that village. If there are not such people, the person is doomed to not be able to get the care they need, like Alex not even knowing he was eligible for Ryan White or Ben being overdosed on meds. In a country where these people are already working at the disadvantage of experiencing stigma from all around them, they should at least be able to come to and trust the people of their village. They should.

Diego

But care is different in other parts of the globe. While some places do not have the mental and social support that good care systems in America have, their medications are much cheaper. The United Nations AIDS organization is what created the 90-90-90 model, so that is not just an American goal but a global one. But, something happens when people start crossing borders. There are limits to where a person can travel if they have HIV. There are limits to coverages when a person travels. For Diego Chaves, navigating these rules and restrictions has proven to be nothing less than a nightmare.

"I never got any sort of care in America," he says, now a graduate student at Michigan State University. He has only received care for HIV in Brazil, and that is a problem he has to face every day while attending school here. The differences between his care here and there are extreme. In Brazil, all of his medications for HIV were completely free. He had his exams for free. He had his tests for free. When he lived in Illinois for a while, the doctors tried to have him tested, but they expected him to pay. Many people have said, "Well, you're a student here, right? Your student insurance should cover it." To that, he says, "My insurance from the university wouldn't pay for anything, for more specific exams or medications. They wouldn't help with any part of it." As a result, he is unable to get tested here. Most HIV doctors recommend getting tested every six months, and he just does not have the means to do that.

However, every summer, he returns to Brazil, and he

takes his free exams there. For medication, his mother sends them every few months. This has been the norm for him for the past four years. "But every single time I take my test, my viral load is undetectable," he says. He has been struggling quite a bit with the meds though. Every time his mother sends them, it has to be accompanied by numerous documents. And the pills themselves have efavirenz in them. Like Jake, they give Diego bad dreams. "I feel tired every day. I feel nauseous. Suicidal impulses."

Doing what Diego does, sending medications overseas, is a hassle at best. U.S. Customs and Border Patrol recommends not trying to ship medication into the country. But if necessary, they have a long procedure available for you to try: "However, if you are here temporarily and need to be sent your prescription medication, there are a couple of things you should do. Ask your physician to write a letter explaining that you are under their care, and that they have prescribed the medication for your use. The letter should also explain the circumstances for sending the medication to you, including, that you are a citizen of (whatever) country, that you are temporarily in the U.S. (for travel, study, etc.) and have either run out of your medications, lost it, etc. The letter should accompany the package and be addressed to a CBP Officer or broker. We strongly recommend that it be in English. If the medication is sent through the mail, it could be informally detained by CBP until an FDA officer is available to examine it. This can take as long as a month. It is very important that the outside package be marked with a statement that the package contains a physician's letter so that the CBP Officer will be more proactive in bringing it to the FDA officer's attention." This policy is what shapes Diego's ability to survive. If that CBP Officer decides not to be "proactive," then Diego does not get his medication. Then, he would be forced to choose between waiting another three months for the next prescription—and hope it makes it through—or drop out of school and return to Brazil.

Many countries however have restrictions and limits on people living with HIV coming past their borders. China, Cuba, and Russia, for example, do not allow stays longer than 90 days if you are HIV positive. Egypt and Iraq have restrictions even for shorter stays. There are currently nine countries that flat-out bar people living with HIV from entering the country, including Jordan and Brunei. Nineteen countries have been found to actually deport people they discovered were HIV-positive. In many ways, this reflects the international lack of awareness of undetectable, and desires similar to Price's: get rid of the people living with HIV instead of treating them. In many countries, America too in some ways, living with HIV means being considered a biohazard.

Sarah Schulman, HIV/AIDS historian, notes how a lot of what is happening in America mirrors issues globally. "At the beginning," she says, referring to the 80s, "when there were no treatments of any kind, any person who had that kind of strain that would progress was going to suffer a great deal and die a terrible death. It's a terrible death, a complete collapse of their immune system. They'd go blind." But as treatments became available, the next question became one of access. "In America, we don't have a coherent health system. It's all about who has the money. As soon as any treatment became available, only certain

kinds of people had access to it. Each group has been difficult to get adequate HIV treatment. That's true globally as
well."

Access, care, village. All of these are integral parts of
living healthily with HIV today. In many cases there is not
a way to get that care. In many cases, the care is present
but insufficient. What can people do to ensure they get
the care they need? Part of it could be a larger public
awareness of resources. Another could be going to legisla-
tors and policy-makers. But perhaps the story only gets
darker from there. What happens when even the policy-
makers see you not only as a biohazard, a risk to public
health, but also as criminal because you have the virus?
What happens to the blood criminals of the country?

4 / *Criminalization*

Alex and Derek

What becomes startling for many people living with HIV is the fact that they are suddenly stripped of certain rights they once had. In some of their initial case management meetings, a case worker is obligated to inform the individual of that state's HIV disclosure laws. These laws, well-meaning as they may seem, are complicated. They often ignore the fact that undetectable exists. They ignore that condoms exist. They put 100% of the onus on the person living with HIV. But, in this meeting, these newly diagnosed people come to a sharp realization: the law has new expectations of them, and failure to comply can lead to extreme penalties. The case workers explain all of this to you because they know the courts do not care if you are unaware of the laws or not. If you have HIV, claiming ignorance does not work for the courts, and the jury is always already convinced you are in the wrong. After all, you have HIV.

While Alex was unable to get sufficient care after diagnosis, he told his immediate family—his sisters, mother, father, grandmother, and close friends—and formed a support group. A co-worker of his at Wal-Mart found out and started spreading the word. His work environment quickly fell apart. Eventually, the store manager had to step in and tell the coworker that if she continued the gossip she would be immediately terminated.

His mom had been working as an assisted living nurse in the trailer park where they lived. One of her friends had been panicking about a family problem, and Alex's mom decided to tell her about her own family problems, namely that Alex had just been diagnosed. "The co-worker told their boss," Alex says, "who then fired my mom and proceeded to call every single person under their care that I have it and was living around them. The old people panicked and tried to get me evicted."

Being open about his status has never worked for Alex. And yet, he started to find another community: a group of five others who had all been infected by the same person who had "pozzed" him. Together they reported the person. The law did nothing. The person then moved to California, and they never heard from him again. When it comes to HIV, the law seems to catch those who are innocent the easiest and those who are guilty rarely. Despite this, Alex holds to his values. "Disclosure is very important to me," he says. "I will never date someone if they are not fully aware of my status."

Derek agrees. He is aware of the law that he has to disclose his status, even if he's healthy. That's about all he knows of the law, but he knows that's enough.

An obvious question perhaps is whether what happened to Alex and his mom was legal or not. In 2008, Congress made an amendment to the American with Disabilities Act (ADA), stating that its protections covered people living with HIV as well. This means that no employer can fire or discriminate against a worker for having HIV, unless the HIV genuinely diminishes the individual's ability to do their job or affects the health and safety of others. Lambda Legal acknowledges that there might not even be such a job: "There are few, if any, occupational settings in which a person's HIV presents a significant risk to the health or safety of others." Furthermore, these employers are required by law to keep that HIV status confidential. And the landlord could not legally evict Alex and his family. The United States Fair Housing Act and numerous state policies stop that from occurring. Of course, the landlord could try to evict them for other reasons, such as being behind on rent, but HIV status is not a legal reason for eviction.

Many people are not aware of how undetectable works, so many genuinely think that people living with HIV pose an active health risk to the general public. It should not come as much of a surprise then that people living with HIV do not have much privacy when it comes to the law. Sally Kohn, a reporter for the *Daily Beast*, wrote an exposé on what she calls "America's Creepy HIV+ Registry." By late 2015, all fifty states had laws that required mandatory reporting from health departments of HIV-positive tests (although some states have started not requiring names, they are still in the minority). While these registers are not public, most HIV/AIDS organizations are firmly against these laws, and they have been for decades. As one study from ACLU shows, this kind of "HIV surveillance" only discourages people from actually

getting tested. While, in theory, having this kind of reporting would be helpful for demographics, the problem
becomes that the information has a greater risk of being
misused than anything. ACT UP New York has an article
on the "myths of names reporting," and they cover the
ways that individual states could force the Department of
Health to open up the names registry at any time for almost any reason. Furthermore, procedures like partner
notification do not actually require using the name of the
person diagnosed, and many anonymous testing sites obviously do not have names to send either. With their being
no obvious purpose to having the names in a registry, it is
concerning that health departments have continued to engage in this practice. *Debate.org*, a popular political issues
website, occasionally posts questions that have public users voting "yes" or "no" and making comments about the
issue. One such question made a few years ago was,
"Should the fact that individuals have HIV/AIDS be made
public?" Out of 99 comments made, 53% said "yes." Some
of the top comments said things like, "They [people living
with HIV] wont [sic] make you aware or give you a choice!
Justice should be dignified somewhere! They need to
speak up. We need to save our children from this life
threatening disease. Wouldn't you want to know?" "Yes,
this should be public information. Do you want your life
ruined because someone who knows he or she has
HIV/AIDS didn't say anything before you had relations
with him or her?" and "If an individual is found to have
HIV, they SHOULD be required to get a small standard-
ized tattoo in a place that would not normally be visible
unless they are in intimate circumstances." People who are

making policy decisions regarding HIV are often no more educated than these people posting online. We saw that with Betty Price and her "quarantine" suggestion and Mike Pence with his "pray-about-it" attitude toward the HIV epidemic in Indiana in 2014. So, we see how the kinds of legal discrimination people living with HIV suffer are often due to heavily outdated conceptions of HIV.

The discrimination that Alex experienced is not uncommon, and it speaks to many higher structures that enable that kind of thinking. While we have disabilities acts in place that in theory protect people, the fact that confidentiality laws are rarely enforced and that filing a lawsuit when you are already at a socioeconomic disadvantage is almost impossible sets up a country where living with HIV, too, feels almost impossible.

Jake

Both discrimination and disclosure constantly come back to this idea of safety. And the question comes down to this: Who should feel safe? The "general public," supposedly exclusive of people living with HIV? Or the people living with HIV? How can we have disclosure laws that also make people living with HIV feel safe? And how can we not discriminate against people living with HIV while keeping the general public safe? These are all questions that law- and policy-makers face when it comes to the future of HIV. But the balance is still being worked on.

Jake, for example, does not quite feel safe yet. "I'm fairly aware," he says, "of criminalization of HIV. I know that it is a felony to not disclose to potential partners, and we still have aggravated prostitution laws. These laws are old and are set for an 80s mindset. I don't feel safe, knowing that people could lie and make accusations without backing anything up, and most likely the law would side with them." While many, at this point in the book, would see how this thinking is certainly outdated, it might seem like his talk of accusations without evidence is somewhat of an exaggeration. And perhaps a definition of disclosure laws needs fleshing out, as well.

So, HIV-disclosure laws are laws that state that any person with HIV is required to inform a sexual partner of their HIV status prior to any sexual contact. This means that the person living with HIV has to *know* that they have HIV. HIV-disclosure laws do not affect people who did not know they were positive. In some ways, these laws are really criminalizing people who are getting tested over people who refuse to get tested. After all, if you are never diagnosed, you cannot be committing a crime, according to these laws. The criminalization laws differ per state, but generally there are five types of wording, according to CDC: disclosure laws that are specific to HIV, laws that are broader to all STIs, laws that increase sentences for crimes involving someone with HIV, laws that punish the same for all STIs, and then "general criminalization" laws. It is worth noting too that "general criminalization" laws mean that having sex with someone while being HIV positive can be considered "attempted murder" as opposed to non-disclosure violations. The maximum sentence length varies by state. Only in two states is the maximum two years in prison. For eight states, it's eleven to twenty years. And for two states, Missouri and Arkansas, it can be a full life sentence, a Class A felony.

But again, in theory, this should be easy to avoid. If you know your status, then you just need to disclose, and you'll always be fine. Right? Well, in 2008, a gay, black man named Robert Suttle worked in the Louisiana Circuit Court of Appeals as an assistant clerk. He was HIV-positive and made sure he always disclosed before having sex with someone. He talks about one particular encounter that went wrong in an interview with Diana Spechler: "One night, he [Suttle] went home from a bar with a guy named Joe. According to Suttle, he told Joe that he was HIV-positive. Neither of them had a condom, so they waited until their next date to have sex. They slept together a few more times before Suttle ended the relationship. Shortly thereafter, he received a phone call that would wreck his life: Joe and their mutual friend were on the line together, accusing Suttle of sleeping with Joe without disclosing his HIV status. (To Suttle's knowledge, Joe's status remained negative.)" After many similar phone calls, Joe pressed charges. "The police showed up at the Louisiana Circuit Court of Appeals and arrested Suttle in front of his colleagues. With no hard evidence, the case became 'he said/he said' and landed, as it usually does, in favor of the HIV-negative party. Suttle's conviction—intentionally exposing Joe to AIDS—meant six months in prison and a spot on the sex-offender registry."

Overnight, his life changed. He suddenly had to be concerned with things like "just showing up in public spaces," he says, "having to show my ID, whether it was a bar, a doctor's office, a bank. The other concern was that I was becoming an uncle. And as much as I wanted to support my nephews and nieces, I wouldn't be able to go to a school campus." And being in prison was altogether new for him, "a place I never expected to be." When asked about the conditions of prison life for someone accused of not disclosing, he says, "They're not very comfortable. For a person living with HIV, it's not likely you'll get the proper nutrients or meals, and also there's the probability that you may not get your medications properly. And some medications require you to take your meds with food, and that's not always an option there. It's really a chance of survival when you're incarcerated." He was moved from a parish jail to a satellite facility. "It was like holding animals," he says. "We'd be on the floors, having to use the restrooms in front of people, no privacy whatsoever. And that's one thing you really have to accept. Where you have to shower or use the toilet in front of a cellmate or in a dorm facility where everything is open, from the showers to the bathrooms to where you sleep." At one place, he was forced to work in the field as a job, "working outside in the cold conditions outside south Louisiana" that winter. In some ways, he appreciated it. He remembered being a kid outside. "But being incarcerated and having to work in the field in the cold where there were men on horses with guns...it was a very unreal experience." Throughout his time, he tried to keep his head low and follow the rules, but during processing, they didn't give him an "orientation" on what the rules were. "You're told where you're going, and you kind of figure it out along the way. There are infractions that can happen. There's a rule where you can't have more than two blankets. Once, I had three, but I had no idea. Sometimes, someone shares something, and you naturally take it. However, if you don't know the rules, when they shake down your cell, you can be written up. What concerned me was that I was close to leaving there, and I was caught with the infraction of having the extra blanket." While they offered the chance to repeal with another officer, the system was still stacked against him. "It's like you're set up to fail," he says, looking back. "For me, it was a waste of time. I can't get those 180 days back."

After prison, there was more to come for Suttle. He started getting involved in HIV advocacy and activism, especially when he learned there were others like him, people who had been wrongly convicted for HIV nondisclosure. Being on the sex offender registry has been brutal. Since his time in prison, he has lived in three other states: Pennsylvania, Washington, D.C., and now New York. Each place had its own rules for how he had to register. When he had accepted his plea deal, he had not been told he would have to register as a sex offender. "Showing up at the probation office having to be told I had to register was very surprising and shocking." He had to go get an ID. He had to go to the Office of Motor Vehicles and get a new ID stating he was a sex offender on it. Then, he had to pay a fee for his new status to be notified to the community. "I had to pay for ads in the paper with my photo, and cards having to explain what the conviction was, and also having to disclose that I was HIV positive....just that embarrassment and shame and fear around the unknown, not knowing how someone would respond to that." While he had a family and a home to go to, he was "concerned about how people would talk at my church or neighborhood. I was nervous pulling my license out for a nurse at my doctor's office to access treatment. I realized I had to limit my social life because I would have to show my ID at bars. I remember one time being asked and just leaving because I just could not deal with that pressure."

When he moved to Pennsylvania, he attended a conference at D.C., where he was going to talk about HIV. The fire chief there started putting up flyers around the community stating that an HIV-positive sex offender was going to be in their area. And that's an added layer of stigma he has to deal with wherever he goes. He has had landlords make him feel unwelcome. Law enforcement officers who just see that he is a sex offender frequently talk down to him. And that's the future Suttle has to deal with. Despite this, he is now the assistant director of the Sero Project, an HIV activist organization that specifically fights against criminalization of HIV. And ever since his conviction, he has worked toward helping others in the same boat as him. If anything, the lesson he learned from his time in prison was that the system was wrong, and he has used that information to do his best to fight back and give others the voice and support he didn't have.

But the stigma and criminalization do not end here. Disclosure laws are one thing, but what place does HIV have in America's legal and political systems at large? If care is a machine, so too is violence. And what happened to Suttle is just one cog in that machine...

Clint and George

Another major factor that comes up in these conversations is responsibility. The current rhetoric puts all responsibility—and therefore culpability—on people living with HIV. The law does not say, "If you have unprotected sex with someone without asking their HIV status, that is on you." The law immediately assumes, even if you take a risk, that there was malicious intent from the person living with HIV and that you actually weren't taking any risks, not from a legal perspective. In this way, the current laws very much take stock in the old AIDS monster trope of the 80s. People living with HIV really see responsibility as being a two-way street. They often believe culpability goes both ways, even though the law is more one-sided.

Clint, for example, is not aware of the specifics of Illinois' state laws on disclosure, but he knows the general gist. "And I don't feel safe or protected from them," he says. "Right or wrong, my thought is the responsibility is on both partners. People have their own responsibility to protect themselves in consensual sex, especially if you're barebacking." George, too, is unaware of the specifics of his state's laws. HIV is not as infectious as people think it is, and if you're undetectable, the risk, again, is zero. A law stating you have to disclose your status, especially if undetectable, is like saying you have to disclose your love of shoes, or your favorite author, or your political party. Each of which has a greater risk of infection than HIV if undetectable. And if you don't disclose, you go to prison.

Several of the people so far have used the word "criminalizing" to describe these laws.

Why do some use the word "criminalizing?" Dr. Raffanti at Vanderbilt perhaps describes it in terms of responsibility and "penalty": "It is not clear," he says, "why someone can be penalized for having HIV and engaging in consensual sex with another adult not disclosing status. The participants are adults and consenting." John Lasiter, the first openly gay candidate for a county-wide seat in Tennessee, once worked as an HIV tester and educator. He sees a lot of Tennessee's HIV policy to also be "criminalizing": "I take major issue with current legislation related to those living with HIV. In Tennessee, you're all but viewed as a criminal. Any misstep, and you will likely face a great deal of trouble simply for having contracted a virus that virtually every human on Earth is susceptible to. There are even those living with HIV who have been registered on the sex offender list, based solely on accusation, not conviction." Carl Dieffenbach, division director of the National Institute of Allergy and Infectious Disease (NIAID), agrees with the larger scientific community that these laws are "anachronistic. These people are no different than people who are HIV-negative. There is no deficit. There's no reason to treat these people differently. The laws and the rules just need to catch up with the science." AIDS historian Sarah Schulman agrees, comparing it to other diseases: "It's clearly punitive. There are so many diseases worse than HIV, ones that have no treatment. It's cruelty." The idea that these laws are criminalizing is universal for people who work with HIV. Case managers, doctors, scientists, federal agencies, media outlets, they all agree that these laws are designed to punish people living with HIV, to set them up to fail.

So, what does this criminalization look like in practice? We've seen Robert Suttle's story, but is that kind of thing rare? In summer 2013, Jeremy Merithew was convicted by a jury of the following offense: "AIDS-Sexual Penetration with Uninformed Partner." While that maximum sentence was four years, apparently since he used a computer, specifically the site *Adam4Adam*, the maximum sentence was moved up to seven years. Todd Heywood, who tracked the case, noted that Jeremy "had an undetectable viral load [meaning the offense of "AIDS" is clearly wrong, as he was healthy and would not have had an AIDS diagnosis], and he was the receptive partner," which decreases the risk of transmission tremendously. "And yet," Heywood notes, "the judge would not allow the scientific evidence to be brought into the case." Merithew is now listed as a sex offender. Sociologist Trevor Hoppe has found a judge in Cass County, MI, Michael E. Dodge, to have a certain hatred for people living with HIV. In 2009, Dodge sent a strip dancer, Melissa Goodman, to prison for giving a man a lap dance while she was HIV-positive. When it came to questions about penetration, this was what was said in the transcript between the prosecutor and detective: "She exposed her vagina area to him and placed it on the tip of his nose and began grinding on his nose with her vagina." And, as Heywood says, "Nasal-labia transmission of HIV has never occurred in the history of the epidemic." The original three charges would have been up to four years in prison each, but the 23-year-old mother of three was able to get a plea bargain of eighteen months instead. In 2016, Corey Rangel, who was on probation (and sober) for substance-abuse was pulled over for having loud mufflers. It was only a minor infraction, and he was told not to worry. "But several hours later," Hoppe says, "he got an ominous phone call: Report to jail immediately.

And don't forget to bring your phone. When he reported to jail, authorities demanded that he hand over his phone and the password to open it." The officer would then go through his contacts, calling them, disclosing Rangel's HIV status, and then asking if they had been intimate without Rangel telling them. This happened with many of Rangel's phone contacts randomly. Judge Dodge did not care. He gave Rangel a prison term for being "deceitful," even though there has not been any publicly released evidence that he had not disclosed HIV to any sexual partners.

But what gets interesting is when the language goes back to "bodily fluids," and when a "jury of one's peers" involves those old tropes. In May 2006, a homeless man named Willie Campbell was arrested. He spat on a police officer and told him that he was HIV-positive, according to the officer. The jury found Campbell guilty of harassment of a public servant. They accused him of attacking the officer with a "deadly weapon." Only three of the apparently over 175 sources that covered the story even cited that spit could not transmit HIV: *The New York Times*, *USA Today*, and the Mississippi *Clarion-Ledger*. He was sentenced to 35 years in jail. A similar story, Charles Clark from Louisville, was already in prison for other offenses. He had been diagnosed with HIV behind bars, and, in 2013, he made a urine spill outside his gate, supposedly to help a friend of his make extra money for cleaning up biohazards. However, some of the urine splashed on another officer instead. And, while he was undetectable by this time, he was charged with attempted murder.

Then, there is the flip side of HIV and crime: when the

crime is committed against someone living with HIV. Near Dallas, TX, Larry Dunn had been having an affair with a woman named Katelyn Torian, a mother of two children, a son and a daughter. When Torian learned she had HIV, as the law requires, she told Dunn. A week later, in September of 2012, Dunn, as one news source says, "had unprotected sex [with her] one last time. Then, while Torian lay in bed, Dunn went to the kitchen, grabbed a steak knife, got back in bed and plunged the blade into Torian's neck, killing her." Her two children found her and ran screaming out of the apartment. During testimony, Dunn said he had believed he already had HIV, that he was already a dead man. "She killed me," he said, "so I killed her." He was given a maximum sentence of forty years in prison.

When Todd Heywood teaches about HIV, he often invokes what happened to Katelyn Torian. "When I do talks at universities with general ed classes or ethics classes, I start the conversation by asking, 'Should somebody living with HIV disclose their HIV status to their sex partner?' Most of the people in the class will raise their hand and say, 'Yes.' I then play the video of Dunn confessing to murdering Katelyn Torian for telling him that she was HIV positive. He slit her throat and left her half-naked body for her young children to find. I turn off the video and say, 'Now, how many of you think somebody has to disclose their HIV status to their sex partner?' Almost no one raises their hand. That is the reality of HIV stigma in America today. When you disclose that status, you are literally putting yourself in a position where you can be killed."

For Todd, this isn't merely a subject of journalistic interest. It's his life, too. In 2016, he was targeted in a hate crime. Two men he had met online and had over for dinner and bonding handcuffed and beat him before taking all his electronics and, specifically, his HIV medications. While Todd managed to get out of the situation and have the men arrested, what they said in their confessions afterward is terrifying: "Seven days after they attacked me," Todd says, "the men told investigators that they deliberately targeted the 'fucking faggots on Craigslist,' because they were 'sick' and 'would not report it to the police.' I later learned that my HIV medications were also deliberately taken in an attempt to jeopardize my health—one of the attackers explained to the police that he took my meds because he knew my status and didn't want me to live because 'I tried to touch him.'" They were sentenced to 17 to 55 years in prison.

Part of what is truly terrifying about these stories though are the juxtapositions. The fact that Willie Campbell and Charles Clark will see as much (if not more) jail time for their untransmissible virus being considered a biohazard as Larry Dunn and Todd's attackers shows that the law treats people living with HIV as subhuman. The reality of HIV criminalization is that by having the virus in you the general public and law-making bodies see you as an inherent offense and threat. Your rights are limited.

Diego

Internationally, rights have limits too when you have HIV, but disclosure laws really do vary based on the country. In Brazil, for example, Diego has no awareness on if disclosure laws even exist there. "I don't think we have any established laws toward it," he says. If anything, the idea of culpability is reversed there, completely on what Americans would call "the victim." "When I go to the HIV center where I get my medicine, we have an HIV-positive ball once a month. We all meet and talk, and I met an incredible amount of older women that were just infected by their husbands, and the idea of these husbands suffering anything from what they did just never came up." While Diego acknowledges this is problematic, he does not see the extreme in America as much better. "I just can't agree with how it happens with HIV-exclusive laws. For example, there are states here that discriminate disclosure of all STIs. But here in Michigan, there are laws specifically for HIV. I feel like it's a criminalization of HIV itself. And also, criminalization that doesn't need to involve infection, which is even worse." Especially with being undetectable, he does not understand the laws here. "Let's say someone tells me or mentions on Grindr that they're on PrEP, and I already know I'm undetectable. Why should I have to tell them? With both of those, it's virtually impossible to transmit it. But if I don't say anything, and the person finds out later that I have it, even though they're not infected, they can start something against me. It's ridiculous. I don't like the situation in Brazil, and I don't like the situation here. They're two extremes."

And he's right on a number of counts. A lot of states in the country do not care about disclosure when it comes to other STIs. In most states, you do not have to disclose a herpes status, even though it is more easily transmissible, just as chronic, and less treatable. Furthermore, most of the states do not care if the person actually transmits the disease to the person—hence, undetectable never even matters. For policy-makers, these laws are not in place to stop transmission of HIV; they exist as some kind of moral punishment for even having HIV in the first place. Larry Dunn never contracted HIV. Nor did Todd's attackers. Nor did the officer that was spat upon. Nor the officer who had urine splashed on him. The law does not care about undetectable. Therefore, what concerns law-makers is not an actual risk of transmission.

Michigan was never an exception to this. The state has for a while had the law that people had to disclose their HIV status before any kind of sexual penetration whatsoever. But these recent events as well as one other case helped Michigan change its mind. In 1992, a man named John Dorn was diagnosed with HIV. He quickly found care and underwent treatment. He has been undetectable ever since. By 2012, he was in prison for unrelated reasons. It was a minimum-security (Level I) prison at Carson City Correctional Facility. He lived near his hometown, where family, like his elderly mother, could come visit. He had a job in the prison, too, which gave him wages and freedom to move around. Due to the facility's open dormitory setting, he could move around 24 hours a day and interact with other inmates. He also had considerable recreational privileges, multiple possessions, and free communication to the outside world. He had around two years left before he would be eligible for parole.

That April, though, he and another inmate, Piotter, were accused of having oral-genital sex. The two men were found guilty of breaking a prison rule about no sexual contact, but what is startling are the differences among their punishments. Piotter received thirty days' loss of privileges. Dorn on the other hand was transferred to the Upper Peninsula, to a Level V (maximum security) prison, explicitly because of his HIV status. The lawsuit that would be filed later says, "Dorn was confined to his cell 23 hours per day for five days a week, and the full 24 hours per day the other two days of the week. Dorn was restrained in handcuffs, leg shackles and/or belly chains, and he was escorted on a tether by at least two officers armed with Tasers any time that he was out of his cell. He was limited to a one-hour exercise period in an outdoor chain link cage five days per week. While in administrative segregation, Dorn was not permitted to use the telephone except for verified family emergencies; he could not send email or uncensored mail; he was limited to non-contact family visits; he was limited to three showers per week, each no longer than five minutes in duration; he could not leave his cell for meals; and he was not permitted to purchase additional food." He lost all rights to the library and even counseling, until a year had passed. He stayed in a maximum security situation for over two full years, and throughout this time, the enhanced "sentence" was communicated as being "indefinite." He had no idea if he would ever be allowed out of it.

Once he got out, he filed a lawsuit against Michigan Department of Corrections. Lambda Legal supported Dorn, and can you guess who MDOC tried to have represent them in this case? "I was asked to testify," Dr. Gulick says, "on behalf of the state, and I said I couldn't do it because I said I believed this was the wrong thing to do so I couldn't be their expert." In summarizing the story, he sees a lot of the emotional aspects that the lawsuit did not even try to tackle. "His mom could visit him. He was ready to go out pretty soon. He had rights to eat in a dining hall and do different things. His existence was still in jail, but not really that bad. Once this happened, they put him in a maximum security prison way up in the Upper Peninsula. No mother could see him anymore. His mother passed away because she was ill, and he couldn't even go to the funeral. They treated him like an animal. They wanted to give him punishment for not disclosing, but the fact was that the patient had zero risk of giving the virus, *zero*, but yet they gave him this horrible crime thing. It may be a misdemeanor, but not a *felony*. There're other conditions that can be just as bad. Plus by making it such a serious offense, many patients don't want to get tested."

Dorn ended up winning the lawsuit, but he can never get those years back. And Michigan has, in lieu of this and other cases, changed its disclosure laws regarding HIV. In early 2019, Michigan updated its law to state that people who are undetectable do not have to disclose to sexual partners, and, undetectable or not, "sexual partner" is limited to vaginal or anal sex, since oral sex poses virtually no risk as well. This update was a major victory for local HIV advocates and activists. The executive director of CARES, the Southwest Michigan HIV/AIDS advocacy group, said of the update, "The Michigan Coalition for HIV Health and Safety (The Coalition) salutes and applauds Rep. Hoadley's effort in progressing a decades old law and thanks our partners in the coalition, the Sero Project for their guidance and MDHHS for leading the effort. Rep.

Hoadley has worked with coalition partners to seek advice and leadership from PLWH and those who provide care for PLWH throughout the state." The team advocacy efforts paid off, and many have seen justice from this update. There are still deeper stigmas to address. This is not the end of HIV problems in Michigan, but we will take our victories however small.

Both on the national and international levels, HIV law remains archaic and outdated. Changes are happening, but they are still taking far too long. People are still being convicted. People are still being sentenced. And people still have to live in fear. Until these systems change, there will always be a need for these activism and advocacy groups. Dorn got his justice, but there are others like him, still waiting in prisons, not just here but across the globe. If we won a battle, the war is still not over. For many people living with HIV, there is still an internal war raging too, a need to feel loved, a need for intimacy. And as you will see in the next chapter, that war is perhaps the hardest to regulate.

5 / *Love*

Alex and Derek

Perhaps, the most common form of stigma for people living with HIV happens in the bedroom, online, and never in public. It is a common misconception that people living with HIV simply cannot or should not have sex and, by some people's beliefs, romance and love. The stigma there is so powerful that many people living with HIV choose not to date, not to disclose, or end their own life. When the law says you have to disclose, regardless of risk of transmission, and the dating world tells you that your HIV makes you less than desirable, your options for partnership seem limited.

And the sad part is that even your support systems can falter when it comes to navigating these ideas. Alex, like many people I interviewed, said, "It can be hard. I've been told I can't be picky because I'm poz. To take what I can get or fucking die." Imagine being told by someone, a friend, a family member, a colleague, that your standards are too high because you have HIV. While Alex always uses protection when he is intimate with someone, he has not been very active in that department. "In the last thirteen years," he says, "I've had two sexual partners. The longest lasted six months." In many ways, his diagnosis has made him a lot more of an introvert since he knows dating is exponentially more difficult. "It's made my life a shit show, and when I really think about it, I get super fucking depressed. I'm constantly lonely, but the time I've been single has made it hard to get back into the dating scene, just to get absolutely destroyed by 99.99999% of people who find out I'm HIV positive. They don't want to take the chance." At this point, in the interview, he starts breaking down. "I can't speak for anyone else and how their brain works, but mine is fucked. I get super depressed, and I find it impossible to do the things I need to do. I'll have a good stint of taking care of myself, then some shit happens, and I fall out, and it's like a wall crushing me emotionally." Because he has not been on treatment, he fears that he is going to die soon. But until he was told about Ryan White, he thought he had no other choice. "I have no close friends who I can really connect with and talk to. No one I can really talk about this stuff with. They wouldn't have any fucking idea how hard it is to live like this. And I understand that, so I don't even bother...I put on this big show when I'm out and about that nothing is wrong. That I'm okay, and everything is fine. But just under the skin, I'm scared out of my mind, and I have no fucking idea what to do. When I die, I'll just be another number that means nothing. And I will have made no meaningful impact on anyone in their life." On one hand, this speaks to the importance of having mental health care in HIV management agencies, and on the other it speaks to the societal systems that make someone living with HIV feel this worthless. Online dating culture is brutal already. Add HIV on top of that.

Derek Williams has been handling things better, but he is perhaps even more fatalistic about intimacy at this point. "I have not attempted dating," he says, "since being told I had HIV, and I'm not sure I ever will." He hopes there will one day be a permanent cure to HIV, so that he can pick up that part of his life again, but in the meantime, he has no intention. When asked why, he said that he is still worried about possible transmission. He knows he is undetectable now, but he is still figuring out what that means. "I always liked having space to myself," he says. "This just makes that reasoning a little more solid, I suppose."

And hookup culture really pushes that kind of isolation, surprisingly. "Hookup apps drive this insane loneliness," Todd Heywood says. "It's ironic. I'm on Grindr, and I laugh sometimes because they'll say, if you pay $3.99, you can have another hundred profiles to look at, and I'm like, 'Oh, another hundred people who can not respond to my hi, hello, or how are you. Gee, let me have more rejection. It's not enough!' That's very isolating. It's very depressing." He blames part of it on ageism. Another part of it is the HIV status. "Part of it is also these apps allow people to make the snap decision and be done with it." While he acknowledges the issues of gay social life before hookup apps, a part of him misses it, especially the intimacy of it. "When I talk about queer history and the intersectionality of HIV and how it influenced and changed the trajectory of queer culture, I have to spend a great deal of time with college students explaining that it was really common that you didn't know someone's name until after you were done fucking them, and sometimes not even then. You might not know until maybe the ninth or tenth time you fucked. And that sexual activity was the norm, part of the expectation."

One recent survey showed that Grindr was the number-one app for most unhappy responses, with 77% of its users feeling regret, with an average of an hour spent a day on it. Jack Turban, a gay psychiatrist conducted an informal study by interviewing users on the app and found that it causes a whole slew of mental issues: "The users I interviewed told me that when they closed their phones and reflected on the shallow conversations and sexually explicit pictures they sent, they felt more depressed, more anxious, and even more isolated." And what Turban is talking about here is the average gay man, not even the one living with HIV. That one little phrase multiplies the rejection count and increases the severity of that rejection.

Jake

Jake, on the other hand, managed to find love despite his status. "My dating experience has been unique," he says. He met the man he is still with today three months after his diagnosis. "I told him upfront before things even got started. He took it very well and was very understanding. He did not attempt to make me feel bad for it or use it against me in any way." In fact, his partner motivated him to remain healthy and stay adherent to his medication. Jake attempted creating a personal blog dealing with his HIV status, but it quickly was linked to a hate-based sub-

Reddit, and he ended up feeling awful about his status and who he was.

One person who has covered a lot of love stories with HIV is Diane Anderson-Minshall, known for her work with *The Advocate* and *HIV Plus* as well as her own book *Queerly Beloved.* "Relationships," she says, "are cornerstones in people's lives. It's always been important for us to think about how to nurture those relationships people have. And how to move beyond their fear of having relationships. That's one thing we hear from people almost more than anything else. After those first couple of years, people are afraid to have relationships. They look on dating apps like Grindr and just see rejection all around for guys with HIV. They can easily internalize that hurt. We want to remind people that they are deserving of love, of relationships, of orgasms."

People like Jake, people with HIV, can find love and happiness. They can have sex and not have to worry about transmission. They can be just as intimate as people without HIV with no other concerns. The idea that people cannot or should not have sex while being HIV positive is a complete myth. And some are starting to embrace the reality.

Clint and George

Part of embracing that reality becomes embracing sex-positivity. For Clint, it was a process of breaking free. Right after his infection, he met another guy. They were together for around ten years. "It was so hard," Clint says, "because he was negative." He had to disclose his status beforehand, and that was a tough thing for him to do. "I went through all the stress that anyone would telling someone you're positive." By that time, he knew he would have been devastated if his partner chose to dump him over his status. He knew he would eventually be okay with it and find a way to live on, but it was terrifying for him all the same. Clint looks back to this moment as being a sign he should have known the relationship would not last forever. His partner had just finished college and had just discovered his own homosexuality. Clint himself was just then learning how to handle his own HIV. He had no idea how to make his partner educated properly or make him feel comfortable. "So," Clint says, "sex was always cautious for him, and a guilt feeling for me." While his partner gave it the "good ol' try," he wanted freedom from having to worry about the HIV. Clint and his ex are still good friends today, however. "But the experience taught me I deserved to be free, and I don't have to be stuck feeling guilty. Sex should be free, and I should be able to express myself." He started getting involved in hookup culture and discovered his own sexual interests. "I love barebacking and whoring boys out and sex parties and different fetishes." And to make things even better, he has discovered there are others with interests like his. "That's how I met my current partner, and we both feel the same way. I've whored him out from time to time, too. I've come to understand that sex has many facets, and people are into all different types of things, and there's nothing wrong with it." His partner and he have been together for over six years now, and they feel good to have sexual freedom with each other. And even his fears have abated. "Being positive doesn't scare me anymore as far as being with someone else."

George has been in a similar boat since his diagnosis. He was shocked by his dating experience. He was always open about his status when it came to sexual partners. While he had one incident where a guy told him he needed to "stop spreading his legs," he had three boyfriends around 2005 and 2006. Eventually, he would find the love of his life and actually got married to an HIV-negative person. To this day, his husband has stayed HIV-negative.

Diego

While Diego has a partner back in Brazil, he has tried to find intimacy here, too, while he is in school. But sometimes, he finds that little bit of stigma. A guy who was in class with him, eight years his junior, seemed to be the type that was out of Diego's league. But at the end of class, Diego got a message from him. Romance seemed like it would be a possibility. But then as Diego started becoming more of an HIV activist in the department, the conversation just stopped suddenly. "I don't know if it's because he changed his mind about me in relation to something else," Diego says, "or if it's because he now knows I have HIV, because that's something I would have liked to introduce to him in a better moment."

Afterword: Hope

This book started out with eight major people: Alex, Derek, Jake, Clint, George, Emily, Ben, and Diego. Four managed to find love after diagnosis. Two are finding themselves, and one lays flowers on the other's grave. The world of HIV is brutal right now, but there are changes being made. There are hopes to have, and there is more on the horizon. And all of these people are keeping their eyes trained on that horizon.

Emily is amazed. The more that she sees being done, the more optimistic she is that there will be a cure for it soon.

Diego is working on an art project that exposes some of the truths about HIV and its history.

Doctors and medical scientists know the medication is getting better. Dr. Gulick, for example, remembers a time when people with HIV had no hope, none for survival. "I'd look at everything in a positive way and try to get them that positive, so that they felt like there was still something to live for." When drugs finally came out, they would get discouraged by the toxicity of the drugs and the side effects. He would tell them there was something new on the way. Sure enough, the meds got better. "The ones that

stuck with it are here with us today," he says. "So I have
patients from the 80s, and they're doing well, and they're
so happy. They're so alive. This is factual. I know the next
bridge coming up is a very exciting one." Part of what he
predicts will be out soon is an injectable medication you
only have to take once a week, then just once a month,
then eventually just once a year, rather than taking a daily
pill. With another person living with HIV "cured" of their
HIV this year (the second ever), the research is indeed
making progress. Dr. Dieffenbach at NIAID has in mind
the goal of making medication more accessible. "I am unbelievably passionate about what we do. This is a mission
to make all these medications accessible to all people either at risk or with HIV so that they are freed and then
can go on and be who they are and love who they are
without fear or risk." Former nurse Mealer is hoping for
better education: "Everybody has something. HIV just
happens to be what some people have. I'm not scared of
people with HIV, and I wish other people were not. I wish
that it were not like it is. We need to have a change, and I
do think education, not being ignorant, is one of the keys."
Dr. Brouwers at NIMH hopes for more availability of
mental health professionals for people living with HIV,
and Fiza Irfan imagines a future where people living with
HIV can have a voice and feel "comfortable enough to
share their stories because it's so needed. I wish people
could be heard without being hurt."

　　And people in the social sphere hope for less stigma all
around, too. Sarah Schulman knows fighting against the
problems associated with HIV is linked to the question of
health care. "If we can get a fair comprehensive health in-

surance in which every single person who lives on this land whether documented or not can get the healthcare they need for free, that would be the best future for HIV." Diane Anderson-Minshall is using *HIV Plus Magazine* to help combat many of the stigmas, too. The two major goals she has for the magazine are to communicate the U=U movement to the general public and to update the HIV criminalization statutes. For writer and activist Tom Mendivil, he fights stigma through his own fiction writing. "When I was first writing through these [HIV-positive] characters, yes, there was a lot of sex positivity, and that's good. I hear HIV/AIDS thrown around like it's vulgarity, like it's dirty and awful. I'm not saying that being diagnosed with HIV is good by any means. But if one does get diagnosed with HIV, it's not a death sentence. You can live a long, fulfilling life with HIV. And that's something I want to show with my characters. These are people, too...Just because someone has HIV doesn't mean they don't deserve love, don't deserve care, don't deserve sex." And even for openly HIV-positive politician Bob Poe, the future of HIV is linked to a strength in numbers: "I hope that there's a cure. And that there's a vaccine. The thing is that we really could eliminate HIV if we had political will to do so as we've eliminated other diseases."

But perhaps most inspirational is Jake's story. Now, he works as an HIV counselor. Eight to ten hours a day, he is working with HIV. He is seeing the face of HIV change. It's not just the gay man. It's people of color. It's the homeless. It's the drug addict. It's MSM. It's women. It's trans people. Yes, he acknowledges, we should work toward a cure, but we should also "address those that have been left behind."

When he thinks of the horizon of HIV, that seemingly distant sunset, he thinks of his own diagnosis day, and how he "celebrates" it, going to an amusement park with his partner and a friend he knows. He's left behind his days of biking into the sunset. He's fighting against the system that has fucked him over time and time again. And perhaps, Jake, as well as the countless others chronicled in this book, who are fighting this fight, are no longer looking at a sunset, but a sunrise.

Epilogue: My Story

With this book, I set about with the task of specifically *not* writing a memoir. But at the same time, as a person living with HIV, I could not write this without bias, as Randy Shilts did in *And the Band Played On*, only getting tested (and diagnosed positive) after finishing his book. And I know, as well, that many of the people who will have read this book—and people I interviewed for this project—will be curious as to my story. So, I decided finally to include it in this epilogue, to obviate many of those questions. I do not do so to diminish the other stories in this book. I merely wish to share my story to show that I am no outsider to the concerns herein. It was heart-breaking for me hearing the stories I did. My own partner can attest that this project generated many tears for me, during both the interview and writing processes. So now, I share my own HIV story with you. Even so-called objective journalists have lives. Mine just happens to have HIV.

I grew up in rural Tennessee, starting in Jackson and eventually moving to Lexington (in Tennessee, not Kentucky). I had fairly conservative parents, but they were not religious. By the time I came to Vanderbilt University in 2010, I would have told you I was straight. Sure, I had been

in color guard in high school, preferred reading and danc-
ing over athletics, and knew all the words to *Wicked*, but I
thought I was straight. It wasn't until I was finishing up
my English degree in 2013 that I really began to question
things. I had been working on a research project on a
queer subculture in Nashville, and one of the members of
that group, a man named Erik (now a woman named
Nolyn), started flirting with me. I was, to my own surprise, reciprocal to this and decided to try it out. We were
officially dating within a month. The first person I came
out to was Dustin, my ever-faithful and ever-diligent editor for this book, and he was immensely supportive. My
family, on the other hand, was a mixed bag. While my sisters were excited—now, "we can all talk about boys!" they
exclaimed—my parents practically disowned me, and my
grandparents could not believe it either. One grandmother told me, "If you start doing gay stuff, you're going to get
AIDS." I told her I wouldn't. I promised I wouldn't.

Erik and I didn't work out. My second boyfriend, in
January of 2014, was a man named Ace. I had asked him of
his HIV status, and he told me he was negative. It felt like
I had found the perfect guy. I remember, that March,
Dustin and his girlfriend at the time—he has since come
out of the closet, too—were going to the Florida Keys for
spring break. And I, being the jealous person that I am,
refused to stay at home by myself for the entire break
twiddling my thumbs. So, I called Ace and told him we
were going to drive down to Florida and take a cruise to
the Bahamas. And we did. The road trip was romantic,
and it was wonderful to just get away and go on an adven-
ture. The second day of the cruise, though, I got sick. If

you can believe it, it was flu-like symptoms. It was nothing the ship's doctor could fix. To Ace's credit, he took care of me. He stayed with me every second. There were dances, raves, games happening all over the ship. He could have left me there and had a great time, but the entire cruise he took care of me. When we got back home, the doctors there could not take care of me. I couldn't keep food down. I could barely get out of bed. I could barely talk. This lasted about three weeks, and then it was just gone.

A few months later, Ace and I moved in together, and we proved not to be good roommates and ended up breaking up. We still talked. We occasionally hooked up. I still talk to him once or twice a year. But that December, a Facebook friend of his started flirting with me and asked if I was HIV-positive "too." "Too?" I said. The truth came out: Ace had had HIV for about ten years and was on and off medication throughout that period. He had known about it when we had first started dating and had actively lied about it. When I confronted him about it, he apologized a lot. He was crying. I was crying. He wished he could do something, anything to take it back. I told him it wasn't going to work, that I couldn't be with someone who had lied to me like that. He said he understood but wanted to make sure I knew that he still loved me and wanted me to be happy. I told him the same.

I went to get tested around New Year's. They said it would take me a week to hear back. On January 7th, I took the OraQuick test at home. It showed I was positive. I got the official test results the next day. When I went into the clinic to get the results, I was guided to a back room. I waited about fifteen minutes, and then a nurse came in. This was at the Rutherford County Health Department in Smyrna, Tennessee. She did not close the door. She just stood in the doorway with a clipboard in her hands. She said, "Well, Mr. Thurston, it looks like your test came back positive for HIV. Here's a copy for your records." I took the piece of paper, my mind silent. "And here's a brochure with more information." I took it. "Is there anything else I can help you with today?" I shook my head. That was all she had to say, and then she escorted me out. It was less than thirty seconds. She did not give me more information or tell me where to go or what to do. I remember being able to hear my heartbeat in my ears.

I went through a lot of the emotions that have been common throughout this book. I felt ashamed. How could I get this? How was I suddenly unclean? What did I do to deserve this? Was I a slut? Was I going to die? How much longer did I have left to live?

That night, I called a family member and told her the news. She and I just cried for a good ten minutes, not really knowing what to say after. By that point, I had been on Google several hours and knew I wasn't going to die, assuming I could get medication. The next day, I called Nashville CARES, the Nashville AIDS organization, and set up an appointment with them. It was so overwhelming. I suddenly had met about ten new people: the secretary at CARES, my early intervention counselor, my case manager, my Ryan White worker, my pharmacist, my therapist, the secretary at Vanderbilt Comprehensive Care Center, and my new doctor. By the end of the day, I had learned my CD4 count and received my first supply of medications.

That night, in the bathroom of my apartment, I sat on the tiles and called Dustin. I told him, and I cried again. I never told him, but part of the reason I called him was because I had been looking up ways to kill myself. I didn't want to live with the shame. I felt less than human, and I felt like all my hopes for my future had been crushed. Dustin was as shocked as I was, and he helped me get through it.

But like the others in this book, I remember the date. January 7, 2015. I remember that date so vividly. A couple of weeks after my diagnosis, I made a post on Facebook, "coming out" as positive to my friends there. While the post is now "private," it is still there: "I know a lot of you will think I'm crazy for posting this on my Facebook of all places, and I probably am. But I am just really having a rough time right now and need all the support I can get at this point. Even if it is as embarrassing as can be. I was just diagnosed with HIV. For those who don't know, my life span will be just the same. It just means I will have to be on drugs for either the rest of my life or until there is a cure, and I will have to be open with my partner about it. I'm trying to just take this day by day right now. Is this post a cry for attention? More than likely. I just really feel that I need you guys' support right now. Thanks." To my surprise at the time, the support was overwhelmingly abundant and immediate. In the comments, people let me know they still loved me. People told me things would be okay. People whom I didn't talk with regularly even reached out to tell me to keep taking it one day at a time. There were apologies and "I'm proud of you"s. A lot of people called me brave, and people sent their thoughts and prayers. And regardless of how dramatic my post might have sounded, the support I got from people online and from Dustin probably did save my life.

Not all of the feedback was great though. I had people ask me who gave it to me. People wanted to kill Ace. People wanted me to sue him. People wanted me to castrate him. Some people blamed it on me. They told me I should have worn protection. They told me they hoped I "learned my lesson." Some told me it was what I got for being gay. But these were rare cases. Most people genuinely were supportive of me. The one negative comment that did stick with me was the idea of suing Ace. I wasn't angry at him. I didn't want to hurt him at all. But if it meant stopping him from doing the exact same thing to someone else, it was a good idea. But we are not really taught how to go about filing a lawsuit, not in high school anyway. I started with calling the Memphis Police Department, where he lived. They told me it was outside their jurisdiction since I lived in Nashville. I called the Nashville Police Department. They said it was outside their jurisdiction since he lived in Memphis. I called a lawyer, and they said I easily had a case. But, the way the case would work was that if Ace lost, which was likely, then he would have to pay my lawyer fees...unless he was unable to; then it would fall on me to pay the lawyer. At the time, I was a graduate student at Middle Tennessee State University and made a meager stipend of $700 a month. I could not pay any percentage of lawyer fees. And from my time living with Ace, I knew he probably made less than I did. Suing him would only be shooting myself in the foot. I finally called Nashville CARES, not really sure what they could do for me, but at least it was a place that could hear me out.

While they were not able to help me with suing Ace, they had me come in immediately. I didn't have a car at the time and lived about an hour away. They had someone come and pick me up in the morning. I saw an early intervention specialist, and she got me set up with case management immediately. They filed my Ryan White paperwork that day. They had me go to Vanderbilt Comprehensive Care Center and get labs done. I remember my doctor at that time, Amen Eguakun, was the most welcoming and calming person ever. He explained every single thing that would happen and did everything in his power to let me know I wasn't alone. That same day, I was set up with a prescription. I had a bottle of pills by the end of the day. I was set up with a counselor, too. And when I was taken back home, I was given several bags of groceries. My own depression and suicidal ideation did not vanish, but they were a little bit better. I felt cared for.

My first medication was Stribild. It was a single-pill medication, and I had to take it with meals. The first few weeks, it really fucked with my stomach, but it got better over time. It is a brutal medication on your liver though. After a couple years, they came out with Genvoya, and I was switched over to that since it's better on your liver. As of summer 2019, I am still on it. I never really had a problem with adherence to the medication, but I have had numerous lapses in medication and insurance over the years. To this day, one of the most annoying questions I get from someone in my "village" is, "What insurance are you on?" My vulgar response is typically, "Fuck if I know." A month after I was diagnosed, I was completely clueless. I was a graduate student and graduate teaching assistant at Middle Tennessee State University. I had some student insurance, but they gave less than minimum coverage for their graduate students. So, I was also on Ryan White. They handled all the co-pay for my insurance, so they brought me up to minimum coverage. At pharmacies, they frequently forget to look over my full record when refilling my prescription. They "single-bill" it as opposed to "double-bill"—meaning they forget to add on the ADAP coverage—and I see the number $3,100 appear on the monitor, and the person looks at me expectantly. I then have to explain they need to re-ring it but double-bill it. They look at the sheets of paper, and I see their face transform into a clear "Oh!" They double-bill it, and we are fine. But the first time that happened, I was without meds for a couple of weeks. I didn't know what arcane pharmaceutical terminology I had to tell them to fix it. I had to call my doctor, my early intervention specialist, and my case manager before they were able to get it corrected.

To this day, I have never made above $20,000 a year, so I am in no danger of losing my Ryan White ADAP coverage. My meds will continue to be covered by that program for the foreseeable future. But, being in academia, I move a lot. Imagine all the hassle of moving that is fairly normal, and then imagine having to start your "village" all over again. Since diagnosis, I have lived in five different cities: Murfreesboro, TN, Nashville, TN, Jackson, TN, Knoxville, TN, and Lansing, MI. Each one required me to create a new village. And in a couple of years I will likely have to move again for work.

One thing that really broke me down in my initial months of diagnosis was just the stigma I encountered. I was open and public about my status. I specifically wanted to be the antithesis of Ace. If I could be an advocate, an activist, I could have some level of control over HIV. I wanted that control. So, I owned my virus. I wore it on the outside. Predictably perhaps, that came back to bite me in the ass. My roommate at the time, a college undergraduate that had been randomly assigned to my apartment, Kimi, had decided she no longer would touch my cooking. She was scared to eat anything I had touched. Being a fan of reality TV like *The Kardashian Show*, she found it was her ultimate purpose to reveal what she found to be "hot takes," no matter how asinine they were, even if unasked. So, it was that one day she approached me out of the blue and said, "So, if I were you, I just wouldn't have sex anymore. Just saying." And what made it particularly difficult, too, was that some colleagues approached me with the same caution. I became outcast by many very easily. Some came closer to me. Faculty like Dr. Cecelia Tichi at Vanderbilt and Dr. Marion Hollings at Middle Tennessee State showed me so much support during this time, and it made all the difference having "adults" tell me things were going to be okay.

I owe Dr. Tichi a lot actually. She was my mentor and advisor during my undergraduate years, and we had this habit over the years: she would tell me not to do something, and I would end up doing it anyway. Her patience with me was astounding. She had once tried to convince me not to be an English major, and here I am finishing my PhD in English. When I "came out" as HIV-positive, she

told me not to be so public about it, that there were people who would hurt me or stigmatize me for it. She was
completely right. Obviously, I did it anyway. But her telling me that was the first time I had begun to realize that
HIV was more than just an individual's problem. It was a
structural one. It was a national one, a global one. And so,
I started to become an exposé writer and thinker, much
like the authors she had taught back in undergrad.

I started getting involved with activism that fall. I had
just moved in with Dustin (and away from Kimi), and I
got my first car. I was gaining independence, and it felt
wonderful. I was starting to feel like I could tackle HIV.
That December, though, I got strep throat. In theory, that
wouldn't be so bad, not in comparison to HIV anyway. My
CCC doctor would be out of town for the holidays, so
they would have to wait for labs to come back to diagnose
anything. The quick strep test came back negative though.
So, I traveled to my hometown in Jackson (about two
hours away from where I was living in Nashville) to be
with my mother, grandmother, and sisters for the holidays. The strep got progressively worse. It came to a point
where I'd have to go to a clinic immediately, but I had lost
my entire ability to talk. While it would be fine for my
mother to take me and talk to the doctor, there came an
apparent problem: What if the doctor recommended medications that clashed with my HIV meds? Or what if he
recommended something that required me to fast for a
period of time so I couldn't take my Stribild?

When my mother came into the guest bedroom to
check on me before we left for the doctor, I broke down
crying. I was so sure—I was *confident*—that she would

judge me or hate me or kick me out or something. I managed to tell her that I was HIV positive. She was crying, too, at that point. The first thing she asked was, "How bad is it?" The fact that she asked *that* question as opposed to a hundred other worse possibilities lifted my heart immediately. She asked me to educate her, and I did. And everything was fine. But for me, someone who grew up in the rural South, coming out to her as HIV-positive was infinitely harder than coming out as gay. As of this moment, I still have not told my dad's side of the family. I am still scared of what my grandparents—including the one who told me I would get HIV if I stayed gay—would say or think.

I learned that year and to this day that people can be cruel, though. I have, for years, been an active member of gay hookup and online dating culture. As any gay man could likely tell you, both of those worlds are full of rejection. It's like window-shopping really. People see one thing that isn't "ideal" to them, such as height, weight, race, age, or an interest, and they click, "Next." For me, that first year was brutal. I had around a hundred messages telling me to kill myself. People told me I shouldn't be on those apps if I had HIV, that I was just going to spread it. That I was the AIDS monster. People sometimes laughed at me. People sometimes told me I deserved it for being a "slut." And please note my plurals there. These were not singular messages. These were not *rare* messages. Over the course of the first year, I had around a hundred of these kinds of messages. Per my political philosophy, I openly put on my profile that I was HIV undetectable. Not all poz guys did that. Many would wait until conversation had happened a bit, and then would disclose. I wanted to weed out people from the get-go. But, naturally, it often backfired, at least on my mental health.

I remember talking to a guy for a good couple of weeks online. He seemed like a sweet guy, and we had similar interests. My HIV status was in my profile, so he would have seen it and must have been okay with it. We went out for our first date. It was a Japanese place in downtown Nashville. We ordered our food and started talking. We really did seem to click in person, and then I made some offhand comment about the kinds of stigma I had received online for my status and was glad he wasn't one of those. His eyes kind of widened at that. I watched him pull out his phone. He opened the app. He pulled up my profile and read over it. Apparently, he was reading it more closely than he had in the past. I saw him mouth the words "HIV undetectable." I saw him swallow nervously. He never looked me in the eyes. He pocketed his phone. He took out his wallet. He laid two twenties on the table and walked out just as the server brought our food. I tried to eat. I tried not to cry.

I had a hookup once where I had communicated similar interests with the guy I would be seeing beforehand. We seemed to click sexually, at least online. Once I got in the house though, he tied me up. It was way tighter than I wanted. I shouted out my safe word. He didn't care. He raped me. He leaned into my ear and whispered that if I struggled he was going to have his dog rape me, too. His dog had an erection in front of me. When I got home that night, I felt like a vegetable, hollow. I did not know what to do. The previous year when I had told law enforcement about Ace infecting me, they had ridiculed me, one officer practically saying it was what I got for being gay. I lived in Tennessee. I knew that if I pressed charges or anything, they would just pull up our text conversations. They would see that I was into kink play and into being submissive. They would not care about safe words. They would see that I had HIV and would think I was probably an immoral slut anyway. They would say I had asked for it. I never pressed charges.

I ran across every kind of hate message over time. People would tell me I got what I deserved. They would ask me what I was doing on a hookup app. They would ask me if I was trying to infect everyone. They would tell me I was gross, that I was unclean, that I was a slut. They would tell me I should have kept my legs closed. They would tell me they weren't "into" disease. And the most common one was that they would tell me to kill myself. And I was frequently told I should lower my standards.

It wasn't until the summer of 2016 that I would meet someone more than decent. I dated Travis shortly after I got my Master's degree, and we were able to bond over books, culture, and good food. He had, in many respects, more knowledge of HIV than I did, and he already knew how undetectable worked. With him, I continued my activism, eventually even presenting at Vanderbilt's Out in Front LGBTQIA+ conference two years in a row, especially about HIV stigma. I would start to write about HIV in my own work and academia. I wanted to fight back. Fighting meant I had control. I finally had a support group, between Travis, Dustin, and a new friend Sherayah. I felt like I could tackle anything.

In 2017, Travis and I moved to Michigan, where I attended (and still attend) Michigan State University for my PhD. I started working for the *Lansing City Pulse* as a journalist and very short-term editor. I then shifted to Michigan's larger LGBT paper, *Between the Lines*. In 2018, Travis and I broke up but still lived together. Despite our issues, we still supported each other in important ways.

That fall, I started a new relationship long-distance with a fellow writer and publisher from Texas, Larry. At the time of my writing this, we are still happily together and planning a Disney trip, where I intend on making him ride the Tower of Terror, a ride that gives him borderline PTSD from riding it as a child. And it will be a nice respite after writing this heavy book. [Author's update: Larry screamed the whole ride, and I was giggling like crazy. We are now planning his move up to Michigan before the holidays this December.] But this year, 2019, has been a year of HIV for me. For *Between the Lines*, I wrote a piece called "I'm Positive," a public "coming-out" story of my time with stigma as an HIV-positive man. The article was well-received, and I got numerous emails about it. Many people found the info insightful, and many people living with HIV thought I was brave and was glad their concerns were being vocalized by the media.

This year, I also gave a TED Talk at MSU called "Being Positive," where I tell some of the story from the *BtL* article but also connect some of my life experiences with some of the larger social issues you have read about in this book. The talk is now online via TEDxMSU, but when I gave the talk live, the seats seemed packed, and it was the hardest thing I've ever done, telling several hundreds of people that I have a disease they will judge me for. Writing is one thing. Telling vocally was another.

But this book has been about a year in the making. I kept hearing survivor stories, stories of people who had suffered from the system in some way. It hurt me to realize that somehow I was not the only one these things had happened to. I had to raise up my torch and do what I could. I remember seeing a column of HIV books in an issue of *Poz Magazine* last year and saw that there were not any current exposés that were really doing well. Most of the best-selling HIV books pretended HIV was solely a thing of the 80s. As short as this book is, my vision for it was a *Fast Food Nation* for HIV. I could not pretend the objectivity that Shilts was able to with his book, and I could not tackle HIV as a "common issue," like Schlosser does food—after all, everyone eats. But I knew HIV had a story, had a life in 21st century America. And if no one else was going to tell it, then I would. Each chapter is only the tip of the iceberg, but I hope that even that is enough to light a spark. And maybe that spark can become a flame. And with enough torches, we can really get things cooking. And one day, maybe, I hope, we can free all these blood criminals. Not just from literal handcuffs, but metaphorical ones too. Maybe we can uplift these people to being human again, as Howard Ashman wanted with his *Beauty and the Beast* song of the same name. Maybe we can destigmatize this very natural biological phenomenon. Maybe we can give these people the hope that they can be loved again. I know we can.

I'm positive.

Bibliography

Most of the sources throughout this book are, of course, interviews. But there were several articles, magazines, newspapers, books, blogs, reviews, and videos that were referenced throughout each chapter. While I did not want to bog down the individual quotes with footnotes or in-text citations, each outside source for each chapter is included below in a rough Chicago style. My partner and I checked links before publication and tried to make the information as accurate as possible, but please keep in mind that websites change constantly. Between the time of drafting and revisions, about six of the URLs below had changed slightly. In a year's time, I imagine another six or seven might change as well. But most of the location info will probably last a good while. And, of course, medical knowledge is always changing. Laws are always changing. I hope that in ten years a lot of this information is obsolete, that we will have moved to a better age.

Chapter 1 – Education

"About Us." *TeenAware. depts.washington.edu/taware/view.cgi? section=aboutus*

Bendix, Trish. "Sarah Schulman Explains How Rent Straightwashed Queer Lives and AIDS Activism." *Them.* January 28, 2019. www.them.us/story/sarah-schulman-rent

"Black Americans and HIV/AIDS: The Basics." *KFF.* February 7, 2019. www.kff.org/hivaids/fact-sheet/black-americans-and-hivaids-the-basics/#footnote-391734-7

Borgella, Alex. "Science deconstructs humor: What makes some things funny?" *The Conversation.* November 1, 2016. theconversation.com/science-deconstructs-humor-what-makes-some-things-funny-64414

Cox, Daniel, Juhem Navarro-Rivera, and Robert Jones. "A Shifting Landscape: A Decade of Change in American Attitudes about Same-Sex Marriage and LGBT Issues." *PRRI.* February 26, 2014. www.prri.org/research/2014-lgbt-survey/

Earl, A. and D. Albarracin. "Nature, decay, and spiraling of the effects of fear-inducing arguments and HIV counseling and testing: a meta-analysis of the short- and long-term outcomes of HIV prevention interventions." *National Institutes of Health.* July 26, 2007. www.ncbi.nlm.nih.gov/pubmed/17605570

Freeman, Gregory. ""Bug Chasers": the Men Who Long to be HIV+." *Americans for Truth about Homosexuality.* January 22, 2007. americansfortruth.com/2007/01/22/bug-chasers-the-men-who-long-to-be-hiv/#more-843

Gray, Emma. "Sex Ed Horror Stories: 10 Tales of Sexual Misinformation." *Huffington Post.* April 17, 2013. www.huffpost.com/entry/sex-ed-horror-stories-sexual-education-misinformation_n_3095039

"HIV and African Americans." *Center for Disease Control.* September 9, 2019. www.cdc.gov/hiv/group/racialethnic/africanamericans/index.html

"HIV & AIDS - Sharing Knowledge, changing lives." *AIDSMap.* 2019. aidsmap.co.uk/Being-faithful/page/1065600/

"HIV and Youth." *Center for Disease Control.* September 9, 2019. www.cdc.gov/hiv/group/racialethnic/africanamericans/index.html

"HIV/AIDS Statistics." *NIH AIDSinfo.* September 1, 2002. aidsinfo.nih.gov/news/168/hiv-aids-statistics

"Is Rolling Stone's HIV Story Wildly Exaggerated?" *Newsweek.* January 22, 2003. www.newsweek.com/rolling-stones-hiv-story-wildly-exaggerated-135057

Kitzinger, Celia. *The de-gaying and re-gaying of AIDS: contested homophobias in lesbian and gay awareness training.* Thousand Oaks, California: Sage Publications, 2005.

Magoon, Kekla. *Sex Education in Schools.* Edina, Minnesota: ABDO Publishing, 2009.

Masland, Molly. "Carnal knowledge: The sex ed debate." *NBC News.* 2013. www.nbcnews.com/id/3071001/ns/health-childrens_health/t/carnal-knowledge-sex-ed-debate/#.XavTGehKiCp

Mirk, Sarah. "The Dramatic History of American Sex-Ed Films." *Truth Out.* June 25, 2014. truthout.org/articles/the-dramatic-history-of-american-sex-ed-films/

Olumhense, Ese. "Chicago records lowest number of new HIV diagnoses in 26 years, officials say." *Chicago Tribune.* December 1, 2017. www.chicagotribune.com/ news/breaking/ct-met-chicago-hiv-diagnoses-decline-2017-story.html

Pagu, Cadernos. "Gender, sexuality and religious instruction in Brazilian educational policy." *Scielo.* December 18, 2017. www.scielo.br/scielo.php?pid=S0104-83332017000200310&script=sci_arttext&tlng=en

Paul, Pritha. "Graphic Sex Education Being Taught in Brazilian Schools, Country's Presidential Candidate Claims." *International Business Times.* August 29, 2018. www.ibtimes.com/graphic-sex-education-being-taught-brazilian-schools-countrys-presidential-candidate-2712399

Pisani, Elizabeth. *The Wisdom of Whores.* March 30, 2016. www.wisdomofwhores.com

"Sex Education Laws and State Attacks." *Planned Parenthood.* 2019. www.plannedparenthoodaction.org/issues/sex-education/sex-education-laws-and-state-attacks

"Sexually Transmitted Diseases." *MedicineNet.*
www.medicinenet.com/script/main/notfoundstatic.asp?refurl=/h
uman_immunodeficien-cy_virus_hiv/article.html

Shannon-Karasik, Caroline. "STI vs STD." *Women's Health.*
www.womenshealthmag.com/health/a19895093/sti-vs-std/

Sigel, Cody. "Say It With Research: 4 Ways to Deliver Effective STD
Messaging for Youth." *The Etr Blog.* May 19, 2016.
www.etr.org/blog/my-take-std-messaging/

Silva, Joanna. "What are the early signs of HIV in men?" *Medical
News Today.* November 1, 2018. www.medicalnewstoday.
com/articles/321920.php

"STD Jokes." *Jokes4Us.* 2019. www.jokes4us.com/dirtyjokes/
stdjokes.html

"U.S. Statistics." *HIV.gov.* www.hiv.gov/hiv-basics/overview/data-
and-trends/statistics

"Walking HIV." *Urban Dictionary.* February 12, 2009.
www.urbandictionary.com/define.php?term=walking%20hiv

Weiss, Robert. *Cruise Control: Understanding Sex Addiction in Gay
Men.* Carefree, Arizona: Gentle Path Press, 2013.

Zhang, Qi. "Increasing Epidemic of Sexually Transmitted Diseases in
China." *China Health Policy and Management Society.* September 28, 2014. www.chpams.org/topical-review-blog/2014/9/28/
increasing-epidemic-of-sexually-transmitted-diseases-in-china

Chapter 2 – Diagnosis

"About the Ryan White HIV/AIDS Program." *HRSA.* February 2019.
hab.hrsa.gov/about-ryan-white-hivaids-program/about-ryan-
white-hivaids-program

"AR 600-110 Identification, Surveillance, and Administration of Personnel Infected With Human Immunodeficiency Virus." *US Department of Defense.* April 22, 2014.

Bernard, Edwin. "The Return of the 'HIV Monster.'" *POZ*. July 27, 2011. www.poz.com/blog/hiv-monster

England, Deborah. "Transmitting an STD in Michigan." *Criminal Defense Lawyer*. www.criminaldefenselawyer.com/resources/transmitting-std-michigan.html

"HIV #LanguageMatters: Using preferred language to address stigma." *Texas Health and Human Services*. May 1, 2018. https://www.dshs.texas.gov/hivstd/testtexas/files/AddressingStigma.pdf

"HIV and Depression." *POZ*. February 14, 2016. www.poz.com/basics/hiv-basics/hiv-depression

"HIV & Mixed Status Couples." *Avert HIV*. June 2018. www.avert.org/sites/default/files/HIV%20%26%20mixed%20status%20couples.pdf

"HIV Disclosure Policies and Procedures." *HIV.gov*. May 15, 2017. www.hiv.gov/hiv-basics/living-well-with-hiv/your-legal-rights/limits-on-confidentiality

"Lambda Legal Asks Court to Stop Pentagon from Discharging HIV-Positive Service Members." *Lambda Legal*. July 19, 2019. www.lambdalegal.org/news/va_20180719

Mascolini, Mark. "High Depression Rates with HIV--and Its Scathing Clinical Impact." *The Body Pro*. June 22, 2016. www.thebodypro.com/article/high-depression-rates-with-hiv--and-its-scathing-c

"Monster who infected women with HIV virus and had unprotected sex with seven others is jailed." *DailyMail*. August 26, 2018. www.dailymail.co.uk/news/article-2018826/HIV-monster-Nkosinati-Mabanda-infected-woman-partner-jailed.html

"More people with HIV have the virus under control." *Center for Disease Control*. July 27, 2017. www.cdc.gov/nchhstp/newsroom/2017/2017-HIV-Continuum-Press-Release.html

"OraQuick In Home HIV Test." *OraQuick.* 2012. www.oraquick.com/assets/base/oraquickfull/pdf/OraQuick_Ho w_To_Video_Transcript.pdf

Peabody, Roger. "Viral Load." *AIDSMap.* May 2017. http://www.aidsmap.com/about-hiv/viral-load

Shilts, Randy. *And the Band Played On.* New York: St. Martin's Press, 1987.

Taylor, Alastair. "HIV monster." *The Sun.* July 25, 2011. www.thesun.co.uk/archives/news/682918/hiv-monster/

Terry-Smith, Justin. "Justin Time: HIV & the Military." *A&U Mag.* July 23, 2018. aumag.org/2018/07/23/justin-time-hiv-the-military/

"What You Need to Know About the Law." *New York State Health.* January 2010. https://www.health.ny.gov/diseases/aids/providers/ regulations/reporting_and_notification/about_the_law.htm

"Who Was Ryan White?" *HRSA.* October 2016. hab.hrsa.gov/about-ryan-white-hivaids-program/who-was-ryan-white

Chapter 3 – Care

"90-90-90: Treatment for All." *UNAIDS.* www.unaids.org/ en/resources/909090

"2018 HIV Drug Chart." *POZ.* June 2016. www.poz.com/ pdfs/POZ_2018_HIV_Drug_Chart_high.pdf

"Categories of Restriction." *The Global Database on HIV Specific Travel & Residence Restrictions.* www.hivtravel.org/Default. aspx?pageId=152

Anderson, Bebe. "HIV Stigma and Discrimination Persist, Even in Health Care." *AMA Journal of Ethics.* December 2009. journalo-fethics.ama-assn.org/article/hiv-stigma-and-discrimination-persist-even-health-care/2009-12

Babiker, Abdel, Alvaro Borges, Fred Gordin, Jens Lundgren, and James Neaton. "When to start antiretroviral therapy: the need fo ran evidence base during HIV infection." *BMC Part of Springer Nature.* June 14, 2013. bmcmedicine.biomedcentral.com/ articles/10.1186/1741-7015-11-148

Cunha, John. "Common Side Effects of Atripla." *RXlist.* August 6, 2018. https://www.rxlist.com/atripla-side-effects-drug-center.htm

"Directory of AIDS Drug Assistance Programs." *ADAP.* adap.directory/directory

"Federal Poverty Level (FPL)." *Healthcare.gov.* www.healthcare.gov/glossary/federal-poverty-level-fpl/

Goodrx. goodrx.com/

Mack, David. "This Politician Sparked Outrage with Her Question About HIV." *Buzzfeed.* October 21, 2017. www.buzzfeednews.com/article/davidmack/georgia-betty-price-hiv-quarantine-question-scandal

"Medicines." *Gilead.* www.buzzfeednews.com/article/davidmack/georgia-betty-price-hiv-quarantine-question-scandal

Sagonowsky, Eric. "Gilead schemed with J&J, Bristol-Myers to keep their HIV combo monopoly, lawsuit claims." *FiercePharma.* May 15, 2019. www.fiercepharma.com/pharma/after-decades-activism-patients-hit-gilead-hiv-drug-antitrust-lawsuit

Chapter 4 – Criminalization

"About Us." *Sero Project.* www.seroproject.com/about-us/

AIDS Legal Council of Chicago. "HIV and Discrimination." *Legal Council.* February 2013. legalcouncil.org/wp-content/uploads/2013/08/HIV-and-Discrimination1.pdf

Bernard, Edwin. "Texas Jury Concludes Saliva of HIV-Positive Man a 'deadly weapon', sentenced to 35 yrs jail." *AIDSMap.* May 16, 2008. www.aidsmap.com/news/may-2008/texas-jury-concludes-saliva-hiv-positive-man-deadly-weapon-sentenced-35-yrs-jail

"Biographical Information." *MDOC.* mdocweb.state.mi.us/otis2/

otis2profile.aspx?mdocNumber=755873

Dowling, Jennifer. "Man Sentenced for Not Disclosing HIV Status, Tainted Jail Food Was 'A Joke'." *Fox17 West Michigan*. June 17, 2003. fox17online.com/2013/06/17/man-sentenced-for-not-disclosing-hiv-status-tainted-jail-food-was-a-joke/

Dunn, Larry. "TDCJ Criminal History." *The Texas Tribune*. August 2019. www.texastribune.org/library/data/texas-prisons/inmates/larry-dunn-jr/1089237/

Forbes, Ann. "Myths and Facts About HIV Case Reporting by Name Versus by Unique Identifier." *Act Up*. September 1997. actupny.org/reports/myths-names.html

Heywood, Todd. "I Was Attacked for Being Gay and HIV Positive. Here's How I'm Fighting Back." *The Body*. June 19, 2016. www.thebody.com/article/speaking-up-after-a-brutal-anti-gay-anti-hiv-attac

"HIV and STD Criminal Laws." *Center for Disease Control*. July 1, 2019. www.cdc.gov/hiv/policies/law/states/exposure.html

"HIV Discrimination in the Workplace." *Lambda Legal*. www.lambdalegal.org/know-your-rights/article/workplace-hiv-discrimination

"HIV positive inmate talks about attempted murder charge after throwing urine." *Wave3News*. February 8, 2013. www.wave3.com/story/21080171/exclusive-hiv-positive-man-talks-about-attempted-mu/

"HIV Surveillance and Name Reporting: A Public Health Case for Protecting Civil Liberties." *ACLU*. October 1997. www.aclu.org/other/hiv-surveillance-and-name-reporting-public-health-case-protecting-civil-liberties?redirect=hiv-surveillance-and-name-reporting-public-health-case-protecting-civil-liberties

Hoppe, Trevor. "The County in Michigan where HIV is a Crime." *Huffington Post*. December 6, 2017.

www.huffpost.com/entry/the-county-in-michigan-wh_b_9602758

Kohn, Sally. "America's Creepy HIV+ Registry." *The Daily Beast*. December 1, 2015. www.thedailybeast.com/americas-creepy-hiv-registry?ref=scroll

"Man who admitted killing HIV positive girlfriend: 'I wanted to make her pay'." *The Dallas Morning News*. October 29, 2013. www.dallasnews.com/news/crime/2013/10/30/man-who-admitted-killing-hiv-positive-girlfriend-i-wanted-to-make-her-pay/

Michigan Coalition for HIV Health and Safety. "US: New Legislation Updates Michigan's HIV Disclosure Science Reflecting Advances in HIV Science." *HIV Justice Network*. January 10, 2019. www.hivjustice.net/storify/us-new-legislation-updates-michigan-hiv-disclosure-law-reflecting-advances-in-hiv-science/

Myhre, James, and Dennis Sifris. "HIV Criminal Laws by State." *Verywell Health*. July 26, 2018. www.verywellhealth.com/hiv-criminal-laws-by-state-48705

"Should the fact that individuals have HIV/AIDS be made public?" *Debate.org*. www.debate.org/opinions/should-the-fact-that-individuals-have-hiv-aids-be-made-public?ysort=3&nsort=5

Spechler, Diana. "Outdated Laws Make Life Hell for People with HIV." *VICE* March 2, 2017. www.vice.com/en_us/article/4xpdd3/outdated-laws-make-life-hell-for-people-for-hiv

Thrasher, Steven. "Mike Pence Is Still To Blame For An HIV Outbreak in Indiana--But for New Reasons." *The Nation*. October 4, 2018. www.thenation.com/article/mike-pence-is-still-to-blame-for-an-hiv-outbreak-in-indiana-but-for-new-reasons/

"US: Michigan Strip Club Employee Please 'No Contest' to HIV Non-Disclosure." *HIV Justice Network*. July 14, 2009. www.hivjustice.net/case/us-michigan-strip-club-employee-pleads-no-contest-to-hiv-non-disclosure-updated/

Western District of Michigan Southern Division. "In the United States District Court for the Western District of Michigan Southern Division." *Clearing House.* April 2, 2015. www.clearinghouse.net/chDocs/public/PC-MI-0037-0001.pdf

Yoakum, Ted. "HIV positive man sentenced to prison for probation violation." *Leader Publications.* June 20, 2016. https://www.leaderpub.com/2016/06/20/hiv-positive-man-sentenced-to-prison-for-probation-violation/

Chapter 5 – Love

"App Ratings." *Center for Humane Technology.* humanetech.com/resources/app-ratings/

Turban, Jack. "We need to talk about how Grindr is affecting gay men's mental health." *Vox.* April 4, 2018. www.vox.com/science-and-health/2018/4/4/17177058/grindr-gay-men-mental-health-psychiatrist

Afterword – Hope

Sheridan, Kate. "Ten years after the 'Berlin patient,' doctors announce a second person has been effectively 'cured' of HIV." *STATNews.* March 4, 2019. www.statnews.com/2019/03/04/second-person-effectively-cured-of-hiv/

Acknowledgments

To start, I definitely want to thank the people who helped me get through it all when I was first diagnosed with HIV: Dustin C. Rogers, Ken Johnson, Cecelia Tichi, my grandma, and my sisters. If it weren't for them, I probably would not even be alive right now.

This book also would not have come to fruition without the support from people like my own case manager at the time of writing, Daniel Burns, my colleagues at Michigan State, Bruno Ford, Jessica and Michael Stokes, and Megan Fontenot.

For emotional support, I often went to my closer circle of friends at the time: Larry Patterson, Travis Abernathy, Sherayah Witcher, Colin Peyton, and Megan Fontenot. Some nights of writing this, I cried. These were the people I came to in those moments.

Thank you to all the people who graciously agreed to an interview with me: Fiza Irfan, Dr. Peter Gulick, Loretta Vaughn Miller, both the NIMH and NIAID, Todd Heywood, John Lassiter, Bob Poe, Sarah Schulman, Edwin Bernard, Tom Mendivil, Robert Suttle, Shawn Decker, Jeremy Merithew, Dr. Stephen Raffanti, and others.

And a special thanks to Emily, Alex, Derek, Jake,

Clint, George, and Diego. You all are the future.

I also want to thank C. L. Methvin, Nolyn Voyd, and Justin Battista for putting together an excellent cover photo on such short notice. It was appreciated more than you know.

Thank you again to Dustin C. Rogers. He did a phenomenal job with editing this, catching not only typos and errors but also helping with my research and rhetoric in ways that proved utterly invaluable.

And thanks again to Larry Patterson. He is my weasely lover, and he is my constant emotional support for this book. As biased as it may be, he is also the owner of Weasel Press, the fine publisher of this humble book.

Finally, thank you, reader, for accompanying me on this journey. Ever onward.